PRAISE FOR MEASURE WHAT MATTERS TO CUSTOMERS

This is the second book in Ron Baker's Intellectual Capitalism Series *and it captures, in a unique way, the importance of measuring what really matters. Ron expertly weaves his logical way through the maze of business information that can, and does, really make a difference and then sets out clearly and succinctly what business is really about—creating wealth for customers, and more importantly how to measure what really matters in an attempt to achieve that noble objective.*

A business book that should be on everyone's must read list.

> —Peter Byers, Chartered Accountant, Byers & Co Ltd, New Zealand

We have known since the 1960s, when Xerox did extensive research, that employee satisfaction → customer satisfaction → profitability, yet the vast majority of companies measure only the latter. Why? Because we have a learning disability, that's why! In Measure What Matters to Customers, *Ron Baker slaps us in the face with a generous dose of logic to help us correct our blind wandering through the labyrinth of lagging indicators like revenue and profitability, in favor of key predictive indicators that define success the same way our customers do. Hmmm, maybe we will **get it** this time?*

> —Ed Kless, Director, Partner Development and Recruitment, Sage Software

Ron Baker has done it again—this is the most helpful business book that I have read. In it, Ron continues his relentless focus on customer value, challenging the reader to rethink their definition of success. It provides both solid theoretical foundation and proven practical steps that can be implemented in your business today to become a truly customer-focused organization. Lead your organization to the next level by measuring what matters to customers.

> —Brendon Harrex, Chairman, Ward Wilson Ltd., Invercargill, New Zealand

Yet more insights from Ron Baker that force us to challenge conventional norms— norms that keep us missing the really important stuff. Read this book and discover that there absolutely is an opportunity to move way *beyond where you are now, into new realms of real relevance—indeed into new ways of delivering a far better customer experience. Yet again, Ron Baker provides a fabulous pathway.*

> —Paul Dunn, founder and CEO, ResultsNet Australia, coauthor, *The Firm of the Future: A Guide for Accountants, Lawyers, and Other Professional Services*, www.resultsnetaustralia.com

From his wit to his insights, Ron Baker has done it again! As one of the best management thinkers of our time, he has taken on the field of measurement and given us the gift of knowledge so we may move ahead as well.

> —Reed Holden, Founder, Holden Advisors Corp., www.holdenadvisors.com, Concord, MA
> Author, *The Strategy and Tactics of Pricing*, Third Edition

Baker's second book in the Intellectual Capitalism Series *evolves the rationale for defining the success of a business the same way the customer does. With impeccable logic, he leads the charge for effectiveness over efficiency by shining the spotlight on the realities of today's knowledge economy.* Measure What Matters to Customers *is a Rosetta stone for leaders who are trying to translate what they measure into value for the customer.*

—Thomas Finneran, Executive Vice President,
American Association of Advertising Agencies

I have read literally hundreds of business books and no author has entertained, educated, challenged and extended my thinking more than Ron Baker. Ron is a gifted story teller who, in a disarmingly simple way, shares with his readers an extraordinarily powerful message. In Measure What Matters to Customers *Ron provides us with an elegant justification, together with a practical framework, for developing metrics that truly reflect what's important to the people who, at the end of the day, determine the destiny of any organization—its customers. If you play a role in contributing to the success of any entity, whether it is a for-profit or non-profit, you and the organization you serve will benefit immensely from this book.*

—Ric Payne, President & CEO, Principal, www.principa.net

Finally a business book that challenges us to get out of yesterday and get into tomorrow. Ron Baker brilliantly illuminates the concept that if everything is important, nothing is important. He shows how to trade the energy you're putting into reconstructing the past and use it to identify the key metrics that will make you successful in the future.

—Tim Williams, President, Ignition Consulting Group,
Author of *Take a Stand for Your Brand*,
www.ignitiongroup.com

In this second of his four book series on Intellectual Capitalism, *Baker artfully articulates why the most important activities that actually matter in a business are those that impact the customer. Successful businesses understand that revenue, profits and other internal statistics are lagging indicators, and that they must look and listen outwardly, focusing on measuring those things their* customers *are concerned about—what he labels, Key Predictive Indicators. I strongly recommend this book for insights about how to determine what* your *customers (or stakeholders) care about so you can begin to* Measure What Matters.

—Michelle Golden, President & CEO, Golden Marketing Inc.,
www.goldenmarketinginc.com

We stand guilty: We have repeatedly recited "What you can measure you can manage," knowing it can be taken to mean everything can be measured. But after reading Baker's Measure What Matters to Customers, *like reformed sinners, we resolved to make more judgments and assessments. From now on we prefer being approximately right rather than precisely wrong.*

—Paul O'Byrne and Paul Kennedy, partners,
O'Byrne and Kennedy LLP, Chartered Accountants,
United Kingdom, www.obk.co.uk

MEASURE WHAT MATTERS TO CUSTOMERS

USING KEY PREDICTIVE INDICATORS

RONALD J. BAKER

WILEY

JOHN WILEY & SONS, INC.

Published by John Wiley & Sons, Inc., Hoboken, New Jersey.

Published simultaneously in Canada.

For general information on our other products and services, or technical support, please contact our Customer Care Department within the United States at 800-762-2974, outside the United States at 317-572-3993 or fax 317-572-4002.

Wiley also publishes its books in a variety of electronic formats. Some content that appears in print may not be available in electronic books.

For more information about Wiley products, visit our Web site at http://*www.wiley.com*.

Library of Congress Cataloging-in-Publication Data:

Baker, Ronald J.
    Measure what matters to customers : using key predictive
indicators / Ronald J. Baker.
       p.   cm.
    Includes bibliographical references and index.
    ISBN-13: 978-0-471-75294-3 (cloth)
    ISBN-10: 0-471-75294-0 (cloth)
    1. Intellectual capital.   2. Knowledge management.   3. Success in
business.   I. Title.
    HD53.B353   2006
    658.4'038 — dc22

                                          2006014055

Printed in the United States of America

10 9 8 7 6 5 4 3 2 1

To my brother, Ken Baker, for his enduring friendship, and making sure I remain humble.

To me . . . man's dignity consists in the following facts which distinguish man from animals. First, that he has a playful curiosity and a natural genius for exploring knowledge; second, that he has dreams and a lofty idealism . . . third, and still more important, that he is able to correct his dreams by a sense of humor, and thus restrain his idealism by a more robust and healthy realism; and finally, that he does not react to surroundings mechanically and uniformly as animals do, but possesses the ability and the freedom to determine his own reactions and to change surroundings at his will. This last is the same as saying that human personality is the last thing to be reduced to mechanical laws; somehow the human mind is forever elusive, uncatchable and unpredictable, and manages to wriggle out of mechanistic laws or a materialistic dialectic that crazy psychologists and unmarried economists are trying to impose upon him. Man, therefore, is a curious, dreamy, humorous and wayward creature. In short, my faith in human dignity consists in the belief that man is the greatest scamp on earth.

—Lin Yutang, *The Importance of Living,* 1998

CONTENTS

FOREWORD

Ron Baker is back after his compelling quest to "bury cost-plus pricing" in his previous book *Pricing on Purpose* (Wiley, 2006). In this book, *Measure What Matters to Customers,* Ron debunks traditional myths that underlie the concept of value. He weaves poignant quotes, theory, research, company examples, and personal insights into a compelling tapestry of how traditional measurement doesn't work in today's intellectual capital environment.

First, he takes on the assumption that resources like gold, silver, and oil have "intrinsic" value and maintains that value has always been controlled by the minds of man. Thus, no matter how seemingly tangible the resource, minds are more important than matter.

He introduces the concept of "negative intellectual capital," which makes profound sense. Negative intellectual capital is where intellectual capital subtracts from value. An example is rigid adherence to concepts that don't work or legacy measurement systems not focused on the right things.

Another concept is worthy of note. He highlights that business effectiveness is more powerful in wealth building than efficiency, and explains why with aplomb. He points out that, too often, measures are all about efficiency, not effectiveness. Focusing on the right measures—rather than the easiest ones—pays.

Taking risk is also part of the profitability equation. Ron also spells out clearly how current measures aren't robust enough to capture the total picture and can lead managers down the wrong path. The wrong measures, or too many of them, can inhibit risk taking.

So what should one be measuring in an intellectual-capital environment? Ron deals with the "white space" between all the quantitative analysis—for example, ability to deal with change, to leverage knowledge, to say no to nonvalue-added work, to delegate effectively, to demonstrate pride and passion. None of those essential ingredients to adding value in a business is easily measured.

Ron does a masterful job of showing how measures can take the "knowl-edge" out of "knowledge workers." If they are treated like robots, they behave that way. If the leadership carefully designs the environment to bring out the full creativity and contribution of the workers, then they become dynamic human capital investors. Too often, he says, the micromanagement of counting trivial measures suboptimizes the potential of knowledge workers.

Ron's basics to effective measures are clear: (1) keep measures down to a vital few, (2) make them robust enough to capture what really matters, and (3) make sure that everyone is on the same page. This book is a valuable read for those who want to use the right measurements to enhance the value of their business.

SHEILA KESSLER, PHD
President, Competitive Edge;
Consultant and Executive Coach
    with Fortune 1000 companies
Author, *Total Quality Service*
    and *Measuring and Managing
    Customer Satisfaction*
www.CompetitiveEdge.com

Preface

Things that matter most
Must never be at the mercy of things that matter least.
The first sign we don't know what we are doing is an
obsession with numbers.

—Johann Wolfgang von Goethe

This book is another mea culpa of sorts, written by a recovering certified public accountant who began a journey nearly two decades ago that challenged his prevailing view regarding the main purpose of a business. In a series of almost unidentifiable and imperceptible shifts in thinking, this led, ultimately, to a profound change of my mental model. No bolts of lightning emerged out of the sky, no sudden epiphanies came to me while driving on a mountain road, just a series of slow, gradual nudges leading to a seismic shift in the way I viewed the world. As are counting and measuring, being able to change our minds voluntarily is another trait separating humans from animals.

When I entered the accounting profession—employed at a then Big 8 firm—and subsequently launched my own accounting practice, I was the epitome of what statisticians call "path dependent"—that is, the older I became, the greater the chance that what I would be in the future would be influenced by what I was in the past. It was not until I had been out on my own for a few years that I started to wrestle seriously against the conventional wisdom of many of my sacred business beliefs.

I was an accountant by training, firmly ensconced in what I later learned was the McKinsey maxim: What you can measure you can manage. This made sense to me, and I even believed it was true with people, not just numbers and systems. I believed financial statements were a vital part of operating any organization, even telling all who would listen that the majority of businesses that fail do so because of poor accounting systems. How self-serving; but I believed it.

As they say, the results of a life are uncalculable and unpredictable, as we make our journey toward the inevitable end. The years teach so much of what the days never knew. The thirteenth-century Spanish King, Alfonso X, said with no apparent modesty: "Had I been present at the creation, I would have given some useful hints for the better ordering of the universe." If I had known then what I know now, like Alfonso X, I certainly would have offered a better ordering of the business enterprise and a deeper understanding of the importance of intellectual capital to the creation of wealth. This book is a result of the education of those intervening years.

The first shift took place in the area of value and pricing, which led to my first book in the Intellectual Capitalism Series, *Pricing on Purpose: Creating and Capturing Value.* Because I chose the path of accounting, value to me meant the sum of costs plus a desired profit, for an essentially cost-plus view of the world. The problem with this view—and accounting in general—is that it is focused *inward* on costs, activities, efforts, and inputs, rather than *externally* on value. It was not until I studied the labor and subjective theories of value and began to struggle with the lacuna between pricing skills and accounting skills that I began to see how flawed my paradigm was regarding how prices are set in a market economy.

This taught me an invaluable lesson regarding the mental models we carry around in order to assist us in our daily decision making. It is one thing for our models and theories to *be* wrong; it is quite another for them to *stay* wrong—this is unforgivable. We need to constantly challenge our view of the world and improve our theories, since we are guided and controlled by them far more than we care to admit. Now I live in constant fear of my theories being wrong—even those you are about to read about in this book—and I have found this is a much safer place to be, as it allows me to process new information and continuously improve my mental models.

Yet after teaching the concepts included in these first two books, among others, I have learned that changing people's minds is a very difficult undertaking. As economist John Kenneth Galbraith once remarked, "In the choice between changing one's mind and proving there's no need to do so, most people get busy on the proof." We humans have an incredible immune system designed to reject new ideas with alacrity rather than to evaluate them. Of course, most of the time this is to our advantage. If every crackpot idea were tested, the costs would be astronomical while the benefits minimal. Yet—and this is where we must strike an optimal balance between resistance and experimentation—if no new ideas were ever tried, we would still be in the Stone Age.

This book will challenge your theories about what measures are important in business. In short, the McKinsey maxim is wrong. The most important things in business cannot be measured, and just because we can measure something does not mean we have the understanding required to change it. We do not need more measures in organizations; we need better understanding.

There are essentially two ways to change a mind: change your thoughts or change your behavior. The Jewish tradition of attaching tefillin insists you bind your arm *before* you bind your head, stressing changing behavior as a way of changing your thoughts and mind, rather than the reverse. However, in a book, it is nearly impossible to accomplish this type of behavioral change, since I can only make you think *with* me, and that is a process of the mind. But both methods are effective, and if you begin to replace what, and why, your company measures, you will be able to alter people's behavior as well as their thoughts.

Most of all, what you are about to read is a shot across the bow of the present orthodoxies of the accountant, MBA, consultant, and rationalist's view of the world. I do not hold back some of my contempt for these disciplines in these pages because I believe they are partly responsible for sucking the joy and passion out of enterprise with their merciless quest for efficiency, as if we humans were nothing but machines they can fine-tune to perform at ever higher levels of output. If this book can contribute to the decline of this worldview—no matter how small—it will have served its purpose.

I experienced a wide range of emotions conducting the research, formulating my thoughts, and ultimately writing the book you are now holding. There was optimism and pessimism, along with incomprehensible and unknowable thoughts, joined with plenty of cognitive dissonance in between; no doubt you will experience some of the same feelings as you read it. I do not consider this a disadvantage or a sign of unclear expression on my part. On the contrary, it is the indisputable consequence of dealing with some of the most significant aspects of business—you simply must wrestle with them if you are to seek the truth. I hope you enjoy our journey together, and find it immeasurable.

Petaluma, California
May 4, 2006

Ronald J. Baker

ACKNOWLEDGMENTS

*Writing a book is an adventure. To begin with it is a toy and
an amusement. Then it becomes a mistress, then it becomes a
master, then it becomes a tyrant. The last phase is that just
as you are about to be reconciled to your servitude, you kill
the monster, and fling him about to the public.*

—Winston Churchill, speaking in London
on November 2, 1949

Before flinging my books to the public, I have the great good fortune of throwing them at my colleagues first, which is why I owe such enormous gratitude to all of them for the human and social capital they have contributed to this undertaking. Thank you Peter Byers, Paul Dunn, Michelle Golden, John Heymann, Ed Kless, and Paul O'Byrne for reading the manuscript and offering comments in the spirit of improving the book. Once again, I have stood on the shoulders of giants, without whom I would remain unaware of my ignorance. I take full responsibility for any and all errors that remain.

I owe a lot to all of the economists cited who have shaped my thinking about human behavior while teaching me the critical importance of developing and testing theories, especially Milton Friedman's terrifying questions: "How do you know?" and "So what?"

To Peter Drucker, RIP, for stretching my mind around the concept of the knowledge economy and the knowledge worker; it will never return to its original dimensions as we all wrestle with this relatively recent reality. I still believe he deserved a Nobel Prize.

My colleagues around the world, with whom I have had the pleasure of working, and who, in the many workshops we have been fortunate enough to conduct, contributed to the Key Predictive Indicators described in Chapter 11.

The entire team at the California CPA Education Foundation continues to take risks by allowing me and my colleagues to create and teach innovative new educational courses, which is a laboratory to test and refine so much of our thinking. Thank you John Dunleavy, Kurtis Docken, Laura Ritter, Kay Phelan, and the rest of the crew for being such strong supporters of our work.

Thank you Eric Mitchell, president of Professional Pricing Society, for continuing to expand the intellectual capital of this vital new business function.

Reed Holden continues to be my distant educator through his writings and teachings, and an untiring supporter of my books. His work has had an enormous influence on my thinking regarding all business topics. I know he is working on his own new book, and I hope I have the chance to return the many favors he has bestowed on me over the years.

Thank you, John Heymann, for our periodic lunches and many engaging e-mails, not to mention your two incredibly innovative Key Predictive Indicators: the Value Gap and the HSD.™ It is always so refreshing to find someone who truly believes business is based on interdependent relationships and not financial statements.

Immeasurable thanks to Sheila Kessler, not just for writing the Foreword to this book, but for continuing to share her wisdom with me. Ever since we first met in 1995, you have been my mentor, and I look forward to another decade of the same.

Ron Crone, Paul Dunn, Michael McCulloch, Bill Mees, Ed Miller, Shirley Nakawatase, and Ric Payne are colleagues who I am privileged to call friends.

To my fellow VeraSage Institute founders, fellows, and associates, who will never be paid—literally—enough for all they do. I am humbled by your devotion to our quest to rid the professions of hourly billing and the timesheet, a goal truly larger than any one of us individually, but possible collectively. I draw inspiration on a daily basis from each of you for the unrelenting knowledge creep and keeping the faith: Scott Abbott, Justin Barnett, Peter Byers, Michelle Golden, Daryl Golemb, Brendon Harrex (the world's first CVO!), Paul Kennedy, Ed Kless, Mark Koziel, Christopher Marston, Tim McKey, Dan Morris, Paul O'Byrne, Tim Williams, and Yan Zhu.

Special thanks to Michelle Golden, for her work on the new VeraSage Web site, and introducing us Luddites to the world of blogging. I just hope we can find a better word!

Sean Kless may just be the youngest person ever to be included in a business book, and I hope this reaches you before your first birthday. Thank you, Sean, Christine, and Ed, for being warped enough to let me include your wonderful photograph that perfectly illustrates how the most important things in life can never be captured by any measurement. Oh, and thanks, Ed, for being patient—and wise—enough to educate a neophyte on the Principles of Sabermetrics, and Bill James, and for writing your thought-provoking essay on these topics included herein. I still find the theory behind the statistics more fascinating than the game, but your passion is contagious.

Peter Byers, who continues to do amazing work for VeraSage Institute in New Zealand and Australia, is a dear friend and constant source of sustenance for furthering our quest.

Supposedly, when Lord Beaverbrook was sent a 700-page biography of fellow press magnate Lord Northcliffe, he forwarded it, unread, to the University of New Brunswick, saying "It weighs too much." A sentiment I know my British Trusted Advisor, coach, mentor, driver, EU travel coordinator, photographer, translator, editor, and Web master of www.ronbakersucks.com, Paul O'Byrne, shared regarding my first three books. Paul was gracious, caring, and selfless enough to take time out of his busy schedule to spend time late into many of his evenings improving this book with his abundant tacit knowledge; my gratitude is immeasurable. I'm not sure why the publisher rejected your proposed title—*Paul's Photo Album*—and my French is awful, but merci monsieur.

Dan Morris, who constantly challenges my ideas, and has provided truly insightful epiphanies with his concepts of what it takes to be a knowledge worker, how debits really don't equal credits (I feel so sorry for his accounting students!), and why accounting is not a theory. Thank you, Dan. It has been a pleasure to work with you this past decade and I look forward to the next one.

To my editors at John Wiley & Sons, Inc., John DeRemigis and Judy Howarth, for taking the ultimate risk by continuing to publish my works in the Intellectual Capitalism Series, and being patient with me when missing all my deadlines. Again, thanks to senior production editor Dexter Gasque for skillfully and professionally ushering the book through production, and to cover designer Andy Leifer for another fantastic piece of work.

My brother, Ken Baker—to whom this book is dedicated—is another indefatigable supporter of my work. When I told him I was struggling with the title for this book, and that all I knew was it would be my shortest one so far, he suggested *About Time*.

My mother, Florence Baker, and father, Sam Baker, for their continuing love and devotion.

ABOUT THE AUTHOR

Ronald J. Baker started his career in 1984 with KPMG's Private Business Advisory Services in San Francisco. Today, he is the founder of VeraSage Institute, a think tank dedicated to educating businesspeople around the world.

As a frequent speaker, writer, and educator, his work takes him around the world. He has been an instructor with the California CPA Education Foundation since 1995 and has authored 12 courses for them: How to Build a Successful Practice with Total Quality Service; The Shift from Hourly Billing to Value Pricing; Value Pricing Graduate Seminar; You Are What You Charge For: Success in Today's Emerging Experience Economy (with Daniel Morris); Alternatives to the Federal Income Tax; Trashing the Timesheet: A Declaration of Independence; Everyday Economics; The Firm of the Future; Everyday Ethics: Doing Well by Doing Good (with Daniel Morris); The New Business Equation for Industry Executives; Specialists Make More Money (with Michelle Golden); and When Debits Don't Equal Credits and Other Future Trends in the Accounting Profession (with Daniel Morris).

He is the author of the best-selling marketing book ever written specifically for professional service firms, *Professional's Guide to Value Pricing* (seventh edition), published by CCH, Incorporated. He also wrote *Burying the Billable Hour, Trashing the Timesheet;* and *You Are Your Customer List,* published by the Association of Chartered Certified Accountants in the United Kingdom. His book, *The Firm of the Future: A Guide for Accountants, Lawyers, and Other Professional Services,* coauthored with Paul Dunn, was published in April 2003, by John Wiley & Sons, Inc. His prior book, the first in the Intellectual Capitalism Series, *Pricing on Purpose: Creating and Capturing Value,* was published in January 2006 by John Wiley & Sons, Inc.

Ron has toured the world, spreading his value-pricing message to more than 70,000 businesspeople. He has been appointed to the American Institute of Certified Public Accountant's Group of One Hundred, a think tank of leaders to address the future of the profession, named on *Accounting*

Today's 2001, 2002, 2003, 2004, and 2005 Top 100 Most Influential People in the profession, and received the 2003 Award for Instructor Excellence from the California CPA Education Foundation.

He graduated, in 1984, from San Francisco State University, with a Bachelor of Science in accounting and a minor in economics. He is a graduate of Disney University, and Cato University and is a member of the Professional Pricing Society. He presently resides in Petaluma, California.

To contact Ron Baker:

> VeraSage Institute
> Phone: (707) 769-0965
> Fax: (707) 781-3069
> E-mail: *Ron@verasage.com*
> Web site: *www.verasage.com*
> Web site: *www.verasage.co.nz*

1

THE CANARY IN THE COAL MINE

*The intuitive mind is a sacred gift and the rational mind
is a faithful servant. We have created a society that honors
the servant and has forgotten the gift.*

—Albert Einstein

Coal miners began employing canaries in 1911 to alert them to the presence underground of noxious gases, because the birds were found to be particularly sensitive to carbon monoxide, which is colorless, odorless, and tasteless. After an explosion or during a mine fire, when it was more likely for these gases to be present, the miners would descend into the mine carrying a canary in a small metal or wooden cage. When all was well, the canaries

Exhibit 1.1   Miners admiring their life-saving leading indicator.

Photo: http://petcaretips.net/picture-canary-coal-mine.html

1

would chirp and sing all day, but as soon as the carbon monoxide levels reached a heightened level, they would stop chirping, have trouble breathing, and in some instances even die. This early-warning system gave the miners the time they needed to evacuate the mine. According to the Mine Safety Health Administration:

> Canaries were preferred over mice to alert coal miners to the presence of carbon monoxide underground. . . . For instance, when consumed by the effects of carbon monoxide, a canary would sway noticeably on his perch before falling.

Canaries were found superior to using mice since they more visibly demonstrated signs of distress in the presence of even small quantities of noxious gas. Whereas canaries would noticeably sway on their perches, a mouse would simply struggle and change its posture, which made it much harder for miners to detect danger. Beginning in 1986, canaries have been phased out of use, replaced by more sophisticated carbon monoxide detectors and monitors unavailable in the last century.

What is the point, you might be asking yourself? Every organization needs *leading indicators* in order to operate effectively. The canaries filled this role for coal miners from a safety standpoint, and the thesis of this book is that your organization needs to find its particular canary for creating customer value.

I realize this sounds like common sense. But as Mark Twain wrote: "Common sense is a curious name for something so rare," and nowhere is this more true than in the business world, where the indicators used for success on a daily basis by executives, employees, and shareholders are the traditional metrics that comprise the basic financial statements—the balance sheet, income statement, and statement of cash flows. What often goes unmentioned is that the traditional accounting framework is over 500 years old, and it has not been substantially changed since the Italian Fra Luca Pacioli published his *Summa de Arithmetica Geometria, Proportioni et Proportionalita,* in 1494, representing the collected knowledge of mathematics at that time.

In the portion of the work titled "Particularis de Computis et Scripturis," he introduced double-entry bookkeeping, a creation for future accountants as big as the invention of zero for mathematicians. The German poet Goethe thought double-entry bookkeeping "among the loveliest inventions of the human mind." Certainly, enterprises need an effective mechanism to account for and measure the financial impact of its transactions, which accounting provides quite capably.

These financial statements were, however, designed for an *industrial* enterprise, not an *intellectual* one, back when there was a more direct correlation between inputs and outputs (wealth-created). Generally accepted accounting principles (GAAP) at present can measure the cost of everything, but know the value of nothing, which is why so many companies in today's intellectual capital economy—such as Microsoft, Google, and eBay—have market capitalizations much greater than their accounting book values. In its 500-year history, accountants have added more rules to GAAP but have not been able to change the framework of measurement to better understand value creation. As Robert K. Elliott, former KPMG partner and chairman of the American Institute of Certified Public Accountants, wrote in an essay entitled "The Third Wave Breaks on the Shores of Accounting":

> [GAAP] focuses on tangible assets, that is, the assets of the industrial revolution. These include inventory and fixed assets: for example, coal, iron, and steam engines. And these assets are stated at cost. Accordingly, we focus on *costs,* which is the *production* side, rather than the *value created,* which is the *customer* side (Stewart, 1997: 58).

Today, we have all heard the famous saying, often referred to as the McKinsey Maxim, named after the famed consulting firm: "What you can measure you can manage." This bromide has become such a cliché in the business world that it is either specious or meaningless. Specious since companies have been counting and measuring things ever since accounting was invented, and meaningless because it does not tell us what ought to be measured. Measurement for measurement's sake is senseless, as quality pioneer Philip Crosby understood when he uttered, "Building a better scale doesn't change your weight."

Accounting reports are, by their nature, *lagging* indicators. Yet what is needed in businesses today, similar to the coal mines of the last century, are *leading* indicators—early detection systems that allow companies to perform their ultimate function of creating wealth for the customers they are privileged to serve. Running a business based on financial reports is similar to timing your cookies with your smoke alarm. The information is simply too late, and only records the score, all the while leaving you in the dark on how to improve the processes that will result in a better score.

Leading indicators require executives to start with a hypothesis—that is, a testable theory about which factors correlate with success. These indicators need to define the success of an enterprise the same way its customers do, and no customer defines the success of a business based on its quarterly or annual financial reports. If leaders want to transform their organizations to better ensure all of its people understand what is important to the customer, better measurements are needed than those from a more than 500-year-old accounting system.

Deep and meaningful transformations come from seeking answers to profound questions, not from more accurate measurements. If companies implement new strategies in order to adapt to an intellectual capital economy, they will also need to usher in new measurements, otherwise they will get nothing but old behaviors. If it is true that we get what we measure, isn't it about time we start to measure what we want to become?

Traditional financial-based metrics are simply no longer as meaningful as they once were. They are a product of rationalists who are able to count the bottles rather than describe the wine. Though in an economy dominated by mind, not matter, intuition, discernment, and judgment are far more important. The complexities of a business can no more be understood based on the compilation of transactions than a human being can be said to be worth approximately $100 of chemicals of which we are all comprised. Businesses need better understanding before they can develop measurements that actually matter. Traditional accounting statements are becoming increasingly irrelevant in today's knowledge-based companies. They are the servants, not the master. Unfortunately, in far too many companies, they are the talisman for measuring success, and have become a tyranny, preventing employees from focusing on the right things.

It is said that it is better to light a candle than to curse the darkness. But in the absence of a candle, sometimes cursing the darkness is important, just to make sure we do not resign ourselves to it. That said, this book is *diagnostic* rather than *prescriptive*. It is an attempt to both curse the darkness of accounting's tunnel vision and fanatical emphasis on costs and production, while offering a candle, lighting the way for businesses today to find their own version of the canary in the coal mine in order to better understand the customer and value sides of all marketplace transactions.

2

THE ECONOMY OF MIND

*Because economies are governed by thoughts, they reflect
not the laws of matter but the laws of mind. One crucial
law of mind is that belief precedes knowledge. New knowledge
does not come without a leap of hypothesis, a projection by the
intuitive sense. The logic of creativity is "leap before you look."
You cannot fully see anything new from an old place.... It is
the leap, not the look, that generates the crucial information;
the leap through time and space, beyond the swarm of
observable fact, that opens up the vista of discovery.*

—George Gilder, *Wealth and Poverty,* 1993

In a world where Google has a larger market value than Boeing and Airbus
combined, and Detroit spends more money on silicon than steel, the old
notions of efficiency, productivity, cost accounting—and how they measure
wealth creation—no longer apply.

How did Microsoft, in a little more than one generation, exceed the
value—in terms of market capitalization, and depending on the day of
analysis—of behemoths such as General Motors, Ford, Boeing, Sears, Lock-
heed, Kellogg's, Safeway, Marriott (including Ritz-Carlton), Kodak, Cater-
pillar, Deere, USX, Weyerhaeuser, Union Pacific, and others *combined*?
It leveraged intellectual capital (IC), the chief source of all wealth.

Yet our understanding of the role IC plays in generating wealth is
not well recognized by accountants, or accurately measured by them for
that matter. Generally accepted accounting principles (GAAP) do a hor-
rendous job of valuing IC, as most of the cost of creating IC is treated as
a period expense for GAAP. This explains how Microsoft's GAAP assets,
as reported on its balance sheet, account for less than 10 percent of its
market capitalization.

Today, intellectual capital is sometimes thought of as nothing more than
another buzzword. However, IC is not about the "new economy," the dot-com,

or the dot-bomb. IC has *always* been the chief driver of wealth, as economists have argued since the term "human capital" was first coined in 1961, and as far back as the late 18th century when Adam Smith discredited the idea of mercantilism. Wealth doesn't reside in tangible assets or money, it resides in the IC that exists in the human spirit; and since this is so hard to measure (how does one measure the ambition of Steve Jobs to "change the world"), we tend to ignore it until it becomes so obvious—as in the case of Microsoft and Google—that we have to acknowledge our old theories of wealth creation are no longer relevant.

THE PHYSICAL FALLACY

For centuries, economists have been explaining the "physical fallacy"—that is, the belief (known as mercantalism) that wealth resides in tangible things, such as gold, land, raw materials, and so forth—and it seems as if we still don't understand this basic economic concept. We seem to think that *matter* is more important than *minds,* while in fact it is the exact opposite. Taiwan, Hong Kong, and Singapore have no "natural resources" and yet they all have a higher standard of living than Russia and Indonesia, both rich in natural resources.

The physical fallacy explains why Andrew Carnegie once stated in total confidence: "You can take away our factories, take away our trade, our avenues of transportation and our money—leave us nothing but our organization—and in four years we would reestablish ourselves" (quoted in Branden, 1998: 35). It is no different in a modern-day company. Its wealth-creating capacity resides in its IC, not its tangible assets. The company that created the yellow first-down line—the marker on-screen—for NFL television broadcasts earns $2 million per year for the idea. This concept may just have come to someone while showering, demonstrating how the wealth-creating results produced by IC have little relationship with inputs, or costs. This is a totally different environment from the Industrial Age, where there was more of a relationship between physical goods and wealth. In fact, 1997 marked the first year corporate investment in intangibles such as branding, training, and R&D, surpassed investment in the tangible assets of property, plant, and equipment.

THE THREE TYPES OF IC

The wealth-creating capability of intangible assets over physical assets is indisputable as we move from capital-based enterprises to knowledge-based enterprises. An excellent example of this is American Airline's Sabre reservation and information system.

On October 11, 1996, AMR Corporation, the parent company of American Airlines, sold (an equity carveout) 18 percent of its Sabre subsidiary in an initial public offering that valued Sabre at $3.3 billion. On the previous day, AMR had a total market value (including Sabre) of about $6.5 billion. Thus, a reservation system generating income from travel agents and other users of its services constituted half of the market value of AMR, equaling the value of the world's second largest airline, owning 650 airplanes (in 1996) and other physical and financial assets, including valuable landing rights. A $40 million R&D investment in Sabre during the 1960s and 1970s mushroomed into a market value of $3.3 billion in the mid-1990s. By October 30, 1999, Sabre's share in the total market value of AMR increased to 60 percent, demonstrating the value creation potential (scalability) of intangibles relative to that of tangibles (Lev, 2001: 24).

While the airplanes American Airlines owns show up on its balance sheet, Sabre was nowhere to be found. A teacher once asked Yogi Berra, "Don't you know anything?" and he replied, "I don't even suspect anything." GAAP's deficiencies in measuring intellectual capital notwithstanding, for our purposes we are going to separate a company's IC into three categories, as originally proposed by Karl-Erik Sveiby, a leading thinker in knowledge theory, in 1989:

- Human capital
- Structural capital
- Social capital (customers, suppliers, networks, referral sources, alumni, joint ventures, alliances, etc.)

We will explore each of these in greater detail in Chapter 4 (and in the third book of the Intellectual Capitalism Series). Meanwhile, the crucial point to understand now is that it is the *interplay* among the three types of IC above that generates wealth-creating opportunities for your company. Human capital, for example, can grow in two ways: when the business utilizes more of what each person knows, and when people know more things that are useful to the firm and/or its customers. And since knowledge is a "nonrival" good—meaning we can both possess it at the same time— knowledge shared is knowledge that is effectively *doubled* throughout the organization. That is why former Hewlett-Packard CEO Lew Platt said: "If HP knew what HP knows, we would be three times as profitable."

Since knowledge can be found almost anywhere, and it does not have to be newly created, it is critical we incorporate social capital into our company's

IC, because defining our knowledge solely by our human and structural capital is too inward looking. The boundaries of a business do not just keep knowledge in; they keep it out as well. Expanding our definition of IC to the social environment within which a company operates gives us many more opportunities to leverage our knowledge. This is why BP (formerly British Petroleum) gives a "Thief of the Year" award to the person who has "stolen" the best ideas, and Texas Instruments has a "Not Invented Here, but I Did It Anyway" award for ideas taken inside or outside the company. Knowledge companies constantly celebrate learning, not just the application of knowledge to the services it offers its customers. Knowledge companies have to do much more than merely extract eight hours of work from their human capital; they have to leverage their minds as well. This requires a different level of thinking and a totally different set of metrics to assess the effectiveness of organizational learning.

We also need to draw a distinction between *explicit* and *tacit* knowledge. Explicit knowledge can be documented and kept somewhere, in a manual or filing cabinet, on a Web site or intranet, and so on. This type of knowledge usually comprises a company's structural capital. Tacit knowledge is a different animal. *Tacit* in Latin means "to be silent or secret." This is why it is so hard to explain how to ride a bike, swim, describe Marilyn Monroe's face, or play golf like Tiger Woods. You could read all of the explicit knowledge—in books by Tiger, for instance—on how to play better golf, but until you actually did it, your understanding would be severely limited. Explicit and tacit knowledge complement each other, as in Latin *explicit* comes from the verb meaning "to unfold"—to be open, to arrange, to explain. Another useful way to think about the difference is that information can be digitized, whereas knowledge is intrinsic to humans. It is usually a totally different experience to read an author's book than it is to have a chance to talk to him or her about it. The latter will give you a much richer, contextual feel for the explicit knowledge documented in the book, and in some cases may even be more valuable. Or consider the difference between reading a customer report and talking with the customer in person.

How often do companies take the time to counsel their colleagues on the importance of learning and sharing knowledge? "He's learning me all his experience," as Yogi Berra said about Bill Dickey. No doubt this gets done in most organizations, but it is on an ad hoc and as-needed basis, rather than a systemized, measured part of the performance criteria of team members. There is simply no mechanism in most companies to reward continuous learning, the sharing of tacit knowledge with peers, or externalizing tacit knowledge to explicit knowledge by performing an after-action review—a concept borrowed from the U.S. Army—on various corporate functions. Because most companies are so caught up in efficiency and productivity quotas and working on their current income statements, they are not building their invisible balance sheet for the long-term—of which the primary asset is the knowledge that exists in the firm. Yet capturing this type of knowledge would be incredibly valuable to the company in terms of leverage, ability to delegate, and as a way to increase the structural capital just in case certain human capital investors decide not to return to work.

NEGATIVE INTELLECTUAL CAPITAL

Before we leave this important topic of IC, it is necessary to explain something that may, at first impression, not seem obvious. When IC is discussed, it is normally done in a very positive context, as most of the examples used are from successes in leveraging IC, such as at Microsoft or with the Sabre reservation system. Naturally, not all R&D projects or new products are successful, and in fact, the failure rate is astonishingly high. Most new drugs fail, as do most consumer products, and books published. Investments in intangibles contain much higher levels of risk and more uncertainty than in tangible assets. If my software product fails, those costs are usually gone for good, unless I can somehow leverage the knowledge I acquired into another attempt. On the other hand, if I purchase an office building or a mall and it fails, I can at least recover a portion of my investment.

But that is not the main point to make here and now. What is important is there is such a thing as *negative* human capital, *negative* structural capital, and *negative* social capital. Certainly this sounds counterintuitive, but it is nonetheless true. Not everything we know is beneficial. Think of the IC a thief possesses; it is knowledge in the sense he knows how to perform his craft, just as much as United Airlines knows how to fly planes and transport people around the world. But that does not make the knowledge valuable; and with respect to thieves, the social loss they impose is a societal negative.

Think of countries that dogmatically adhere to the principles of socialism or Marxism, even though both of these theories of social organization have been repudiated by empirical evidence. There has been enormous negative social capital built up over the past five decades in Castro's Cuba, just as there was in the former Soviet Union. As the latter struggles to make its transition to a free-market economy, these negative legacies are being felt (lack of secure private property rights, no effective system of jurisprudence to adjudicate disputes, no effective banking and credit system and other institutions necessary for economic growth). When president Ronald Reagan was asked what he thought of the Berlin Wall during a visit to Germany, he gestured at the Wall and said succinctly, "It's as ugly as the idea behind it" (Morris, 1999: 461).

Examples of negative intellectual capital in an organization would include a rigid adherence to old methods that are hindering your people from achieving their potential, and subtracting from value creation. High on this list would include cost-plus pricing, Industrial Age efficiency metrics, focusing on activities and costs rather than results and value, and other forms of negative IC that have embedded themselves into the culture. These negative ideas have permeated each type of knowledge discussed herein—human, structural, and certainly social—and have become part of our tacit and explicit knowledge systems. One of the duties of this book is to point out how these legacy systems are indeed *negative* forms of IC and need to be replaced in the knowledge company of the future.

Throughout history, the physical fallacy was an idea that reigned supreme, that is, the notion that wealth is embedded in physical tangible assets. Economists now have a far better understanding of how wealth is created from free minds operating in free markets, which can be seen by observing various developing economies escaping the shackles of poverty, creating wealth and a better standard of living for their populations. It is now clear that approximately 75 percent of the wealth-creating capacity of a country resides in human capital, and economists have proven this at the macro level of economic organization. What is needed now is to apply these same ideas at the micro level of the business entity by positing a new theory for the intellectual capital company of the future.

Before we do, though, let us examine the old theory of the company so we can improve upon it.

3

THE OLD BUSINESS EQUATION

A theory that cannot be refuted is not scientific.

—Karl Popper

Theories are powerful because they seek to do one of three things: explain, predict, or prescribe. Yet, when one reads a typical business book today, the author will usually begin by saying something to the effect that "this book is not based on some 'ivory tower' theoretical model, but on practical, real-world experience and examples." Beware when you read such a qualifier, because, as Dr. W. Edwards Demming used to say, "No theory, no learning." In a business environment, whether we know it or not, we are guided to a great degree by theoretical constructs that have evolved in order to simplify—and thus explain, predict or control—our various behaviors. As Immanuel Kant said "Concepts without perceptions are empty; perceptions without concepts are blind." Theories build buildings, bridges, fly airplanes, and put men on the moon.

Indeed, the purpose of this chapter is to examine the flaws in the old theory of the Industrial Age enterprise in order to construct a better theory for today's intellectual capital enterprise. In general, the theory that originally explained the Wright brothers' flying machine has been significantly enhanced by Boeing in order to keep its 777 in the air. This is how theories and knowledge progress—and they can have an enormous impact on our behavior. So even though discussing theory may be much maligned in today's business environment, I believe all learning starts with theory, and thus we will now critically examine the predominant theory of the Industrial Age organization.

"ANALYZING" THE PREDOMINANT BUSINESS EQUATION

In Greek language, "analyze" means "to unloosen, separate into parts," which we will proceed to do with this theory before positing a better theory. When you think about the traditional theory of an enterprise, you would no doubt construct a model similar to this:

$$\text{Revenue} = \text{Capacity} \times \text{Efficiency} \times \text{Cost-Plus Price}$$

Since this model dominates the thinking of business leaders to this day, it is worth explaining it in greater detail in order to understand both its strengths and—as will be increasingly detailed—its fundamental weaknesses.

Consider a professional service firm—such as accounting, legal, architecture, engineering, consulting, advertising, and so on—the archetypal pyramid firm model rested on the foundation of leveraging people power, in effect their "capacity." The theory is this: Since the two main drivers of profitability are leverage (number of team members per owner and the hourly rate realization, a form of cost-plus pricing), if each partner could oversee a group of professionals, this would provide the firm with additional capacity to generate top-line revenue, and thus add to the profitability and size of the firm. If a firm wanted to add to its revenue base, it had two primary choices: it could work its people more hours or it could hire more people. It is no secret which choice the average firm tends to choose, much to the chagrin of its already overworked team members. In most firms, the partners wait till demand is bursting at the seams before they add more professionals.

Now compare this practice with respect to capacity in other industries— this process of adding capacity *after* revenue is backward. If you think of any other industry or company—from Intel to General Electric, from FedEx to Microsoft—capacity is almost always added *before* revenue. Consider specifically FedEx: Before Fred Smith could deliver his first overnight package, he had to have trucks, drivers, airplanes, and facilities throughout the country, all at enormous fixed costs (indeed, those large fixed costs almost bankrupted FedEx in the early days). Most organizations operate with capacity to spare, which is vital to maintaining flexibility in changing market conditions.

Next, let us look at the second element in the old theory—efficiency. Efficiency is a word that can be said with perfect impunity, since no one in their right mind would dispute the goal of operating efficiently. In fact, it is well known that in free market economies, efficiency is critical, as it ensures a society's resources are not going to waste. It is also well established that different levels of productivity largely explain differences in wages across countries. An American farmer will earn more plowing with a tractor than a Cuban farmer with an ox and hand plow; the American farmer is more productive, hence higher wages and more profits.

There is no doubt that increasing efficiency—or at least not sliding into inefficiency—is important. But the pendulum has swung too far in the direction of efficiency over everything else. It seems innovation, dynamism, customer service, investments in human capital, and effectiveness have all been sacrificed on the altar of efficiency. It is critical to bear in mind that a business does not exist to be efficient; rather, it exists to create wealth for its customers. This wealth creation function can be thought of as the difference between the maximum price a customer would be willing to pay minus the opportunity costs of the activities necessary to bring to market the product or service.

Peter Drucker was fond of pointing out that the last buggy-whip manufacturers were models of efficiency. So what? What happens if you are efficient at doing the wrong things? That cannot be labeled progress. In fact, one indicator an industry is in the mature or decline stage of the product/service life cycle is when it is at the apogee of its theoretical level of efficiency.

The point is this: In industry after industry, the history of economic progress has not been to wring out the last 5 to 10 percent of efficiency, but rather to change the model to more effectively create wealth. From Walt Disney and Fred Smith to Bill Gates and Larry Ellison, these entrepreneurs did not get where they are by focusing on efficiency. All of these entrepreneurs created enormous wealth by delivering more effectively what customers were willing to pay for.

Next is cost-plus pricing, a direct cousin of the Dupont return on investment formula. But the real ancestor of cost-plus pricing is the Labor Theory of Value, posited by economists of the eighteenth century and Karl Marx in the middle nineteenth. This theory was almost immediately shown to be false—in terms of its ability to explain, predict, or prescribe—as a method of determining value in a marketplace. Fortunately, a better theory was posited, known as the Subjective Theory of Value—that is, ultimately, the person paying for an item, not the seller's internal overhead, desired profit, or labor hours, determines the value of anything. Value, like beauty, is in the eye of the beholder.

The offense of believing internal costs have anything to do with value is serious. A business should be judged—and price-based—on the results and wealth it creates for its customers. The cost-plus pricing paradigm is not worthy of businesses operating in an intellectual capital economy, and it is time we throw it on the ash heap of history. It is an idea from the day before yesterday. This topic is covered in depth in the first book of the Intellectual Capitalism Series, *Pricing on Purpose: Creating and Capturing Value.*

Last, consider revenue. It is one thing to get *more* business; it is quite another to get *better* business. The "bigger is better" mentality is an empty promise for most companies. Acquiring more customers is not necessarily better. Growth simply for the sake of growth is the ideology of the cancer cell, not a strategy for a viable, profitable company. It is worth looking at the historical origins of this market share myth. In the late 1800s and early 1900s, market share theory was an excellent rationale for antitrust enforcements. You can certainly see it in the algebraic effect of greater revenue in the equation. Once fixed costs are covered, any marginal revenue will contribute to the bottom line. Of course, this implicitly implies any customer is a good customer, which is certainly a debatable proposition.

One widely quoted study is that of Harvard Business School professor Robert D. Buzzell, who, in 1975, published an article in *Harvard Business Review,* "Market Share—A Key to Profitability." This article provided empirical evidence that companies that had dominant market share had higher profitability levels. Of course, if one is not grounded in theory, then it is easier to confuse cause and effect by merely observing the manifestations of a competitive advantage. Height and weight are closely associated but you won't grow taller by eating more. Market share is the *result* of a sustainable competitive advantage, not the *cause.*

If market share explained profitability, General Motors, United Airlines, Sears, and Philips should be the most profitable companies in their respective industries. Yet they have all turned in mediocre profitability records. Growth in profitability usually precedes market share, not vice versa. Wal-Mart, for example, was far more profitable than Sears, long before it had a sizeable market share. It seems profitability and market share grow in tandem with a viable value proposition customers are willing to pay for. The road to hell is paved with the pursuit of volume. Don't make this mistake. More often than not, less is more.

I have exposed some of the flaws of the traditional Industrial Era business equation. Although this discussion is not meant to be comprehensive, it nevertheless sets forth a compelling case against the old theory. Is there a better theory, one that takes into account the real wealth-producing capacity and other critical success factors of the business of the future? It is a valuable accomplishment to point out defects in a theory—or falsify it entirely—but the real work begins by constructing a new theory, as this is how all knowledge advances.

4

THE NEW BUSINESS EQUATION

Models and theories exist to guide managerial judgment,
not replace it.

—John Kay, *Foundations of Corporate Success,* 1995

The old equation is no longer relevant to the drivers of success in the business of the future. Buckminster Fuller (designer, cosmologist, philosopher, mathematician, and architect—he designed the geodesic dome) once said, "You can't change anything by fighting or resisting it. You change something by making it obsolete through superior methods." It is time to replace the old equation described in the previous chapter with this new model:

Profitability = Intellectual Capital × Price × Effectiveness

Let us explore each component of this equation; then we will discuss why it is a better theory for explaining the success of companies operating in today's marketplace.

We start with profitability, rather than revenue, because we are not interested in growth merely for the sake of growth. As many companies around the world have learned—some the hard way, such as the airlines, retailers, and automobile manufacturers—market share is not the open sesame to more profitability. We are interested in finding the right customer, at the right price, consistent with our vision and mission, even if that means frequently turning away customers. I have coined a corollary to Gresham's law—bad money drives out good—from monetary economics, affectionately known as Baker's Law: *Bad customers drive out good customers.*

Adopting this belief means you need to become much more selective about whom you do business with; even though that marginal business may be "profitable" by conventional accounting standards. Very often the most important costs—and benefits, for that matter—don't ever show up on a profit and loss statement. Accepting customers who are not a good fit for your company—either because of their personality or the nature of the work involved—has many deleterious effects, such as negatively affecting team member morale and committing fixed capacity to customers who do not value your offerings. This is why the new equation focuses on profitability, not simply gross revenue. When it comes to customers, less is usually more.

As pointed out in Chapter 2, for our purposes in this book, intellectual capital is comprised of three primary components:

1. **Human capital (HC).** This comprises your team members and associates who work either for you or with you. As one industry leader said, this is the capital that leaves in the elevator at night. The important thing to remember about HC is it cannot be owned, only contracted, since it is completely volitional. In fact, more and more, knowledge workers own the means of your company's production, and knowledge workers will invest their HC in those organizations that pay a decent return on investment, both economic and psychological. In the final analysis, your people are not assets (they deserve more respect than a copier machine and a computer), they are not resources to be harvested from the land like coal when you run out; ultimately, they are *volunteers* and it is totally up to them whether or not they get back into the elevator the following morning.

2. **Structural capital.** This is everything that remains in your company once the HC has stepped into the elevator, such as databases, customer lists, systems, procedures, intranets, manuals, files, technology, and all of the explicit knowledge tools you utilize in order to produce results for your customers.

3. **Social capital.** This includes your customers, the main reason a business exists; but it also includes your suppliers, vendors, networks, referral sources, alumni, joint venture and alliance partners, and reputation. Of the three types of IC, this is perhaps the least leveraged, and yet it is highly valued by customers.

Wealth does not exist in tangible resources—such as timber, land, real estate, oil, and so forth—but in ideas and their creative expression. Oil was completely useless—in fact, if you were a farmer, it was an absolute nuisance—until the combustion engine was invented from the mind of man.

For too long, companies have let their prices be solely or largely predicated on an arbitrary rule of thumb, competitors' prices, or on an overhead plus desired net income calculation. These pricing mechanisms are relics of Karl Marx's Labor Theory of Value and are completely obsolete in an intellectual capital, innovative, and dynamic economy.

In the business of the future, *effectiveness* takes precedence over efficiency. A business does not exist to be efficient; it exists to create wealth for its customers. An obsessive compulsion to increase efficiency (doing things right) reduces the firm's effectiveness at doing the right things. The pursuit of efficiency has hindered most companies' capability to pursue opportunities, hence these organizations spend most of their time solving problems. One cannot grow a company and continuously cut costs and increase efficiency.

It is not that efficiency is bad, per se, it is that it is being pursued at the expense of nearly everything else. To add insult to injury, the efficiency measures that do exist in the modern organization tend to be *lagging* indicators that measure efforts and activities, not *leading* indicators that measure results and define success the same way the customer does. Focusing on effectiveness implicitly recognizes there is no such thing as a free statistic. Just because we can measure something accurately does not mean we should. Effectiveness means that imprecise measurements of the *right* things are infinitely more valuable than precise measurements of the *wrong* things. This will no doubt shock some readers, especially those who were trained in cost accounting or possess MBAs. But controlling costs, and accounting for them, does not ensure success. Companies are not machines subject to the laws of electromechanical engineering. They are composed of human beings who do not check their emotions at the door, and they are subject to fears, doubts, variable levels of self-esteem, uncertainty, anger, rage, and a whole range of other emotions that cannot be captured by traditional efficiency measurements. In other words, *humans are messy.* Focusing on effectiveness does not eliminate these issues, but it does take them into account far better than efficiency metrics, which can be desensitizing and inhumane at times.

This new equation comports with the realities of an intellectual capital economy, taking into account knowledge workers who use their hearts and minds, not their brawn and hands. This equation recognizes the importance of mind over matter, the price thereof, and the effectiveness of the workers who produce it, as well as the customers who purchase it. It may not yet be a perfect theory, but it is far superior to the alternative discussed in the prior chapter.

COGNITIVE DISSONANCE

I am going to rely on the readers' ability to hold two opposite thoughts in their head at the same time, while still functioning. I have a love/hate relationship with the preceding equation. On the one hand, it is a superior model for the business of the future because it recognizes the realities of the marketplace in which companies operate, and it focuses on leveraging the right things. It takes into account the importance of dynamism, innovation, and a whole host of other human activities that are simply not captured in the old equation. On the other hand, because it is nothing more than an algebraic equation, it is an incredible simplification of the components that comprise the typical organization. When we look at equations we tend to think of each component comprising a separate part that can be individually manipulated and controlled, a very one-dimensional view of a business made up of human beings. What the equation does not explain is *how* to raise prices, or *how* to increase effectiveness, nor does it explain the interconnections and interdependencies of the various components. Certainly the equation can describe an abstract feature such as effectiveness, but it does not really enhance one's understanding of how change occurs in the firm as a whole. In other words, it can explain the *ends* (profitability), but not the *means* (how does one measure effectiveness?).

Any equation assumes a certain cause-and-effect relationship, and tends to lead us to believe these patterns are sequential and linear and not subject to the perpetual feedback of prior causes. In the old equation, increase capacity and revenue grows; in the day-to-day realities of a company, trying to work your team members more hours is going to have a whole host of unintended consequences that will ultimately effect the goal of increasing profit. No equation can capture the richness of these interrelated means.

Another problem with the equation is it presents the characteristics of a firm as nothing but the sum of the parts; if you change one aspect, you invariably change another by an equal amount. But in a living, breathing, organic system such as a firm, parts and wholes are not linked so linearly. Thus a small change in one of the parts can have a profound and dramatic influence on everything else. Think of the effects of a toxic manager who belittles and intimidates his team members. He may achieve higher efficiency in one aspect of the equation, and so totally destroy morale and motivation that the ultimate outcome will be a reduction in firm effectiveness, customer service, and profitability.

Peter Drucker has left business executives a rich legacy in his writings, extensively detailing why traditional management science fails to perform. Executives who believe they can change one aspect of a company without affecting others are ignoring the reality of a firm being an *interdependent* system. Drucker explained the phenomenon this way:

> There is one fundamental insight underlying all management science.
> It is that the business enterprise is a *system* of the highest order: a system

whose parts are human beings contributing voluntarily of their knowledge, skill and dedication to a joint venture. And one thing characterizes all genuine systems, whether they be mechanical like the control of a missile, biological like a tree, or social like the business enterprise: it is interdependence. The whole of a system is not necessarily improved if one particular function or part is improved or made more efficient. In fact, the system may well be damaged thereby, or even destroyed. In some cases the best way to strengthen the system may be to weaken a part—to make it less precise or less efficient. For what matters in any system is the performance of the whole; this is the result of growth and of dynamic balance, adjustment, and integration, rather than of mere technical efficiency.

Primary emphasis on the efficiency of parts in management science is therefore bound to do damage. It is bound to optimize precision of the tool at the expense of the health and performance of the whole (Drucker, 2004: 97).

Any equation is similar to the difference between a map and a territory; one is a two-dimensional explanation and the other is full of complex and rich interconnections that could never be captured on paper. It has been said the difference between studying a living entity on paper is like performing an autopsy on dolphins versus swimming with them. Certainly both activities will give you a better understanding of dolphins, but which one will let you observe the rich and contextual feel of a living creature? Clinical pathologists implicitly understand this difference, as they instruct physicians to never treat a test result but rather treat the patient.

The careful reader—perhaps the reader with scientific or marketing training—will note the equation doesn't answer the important question of why we are in business, as it appears to put profitability above all else. This is a serious omission. The fact that a business needs to make a profit is a tautology, and is in fact quite irrelevant. Most importantly, a business must create and retain customers and add wealth to their lives by providing them more in value than the price they are paying. The equation also does not answer the all-important question: Where are profits derived from? This we will discuss in the next section.

One more criticism of this equation should be mentioned before we leave this analysis. The word "efficiency" has been deliberately replaced with "effectiveness," bowing to the observation that a business does not exist to be efficient, but rather effective. What happens if you are 100 percent efficient at doing the *wrong* thing? Effectiveness, on the other hand, stresses the power to produce a particular effect, in this case, something of value for customers. Still, this word, too, is not quite precise enough at describing the effect a modern firm is trying to create. I much prefer the word "efficacious," meaning having the power to produce a desired effect. This term is used to describe the miraculous power of many drugs, since it suggests possession of a special quality or virtue that makes it possible to achieve a result. In an intellectual capital economy, where wealth is created using the power of the mind—as opposed to the body—these characteristics better explain the value created by knowledge workers.

In any event, while one could point out other weaknesses in the new equation, in a book we must break things down into separate components in order to deal with them more effectively. We cannot do everything at once. This is the advantage of a theory, because while it will never capture the true essence of a living organization, it can be studied in its quantitative and qualitative parts, advancing our understanding of how those parts are interdependent. A theory need not be elegant (Einstein quipped, "elegance is for tailors"), nor capture the entire essence of the phenomena it is trying to explain; all it is has to do to be effective is allow us to predict, explain, or prescribe the behavior we observe. It is similar to a camera, not a photograph, in that it is a tool that can be used well or badly, to capture reality, not depict it.

Another important element of theory building is to have a preference to shave with Occam's razor—that is, any hypothesis must not be developed beyond necessity. Unfortunately, most business books contain a paucity of theory, and when they do, the razor couldn't cut butter. To this end, the new equation is presented only as a model—a map—to help us capture a deeper understanding of how organizations can operate more effectively in an intellectual capital economy. No one would argue you can get anywhere by looking at maps without venturing out to sea. But no one would suggest you would be very safe at sea without a map.

WHERE DO PROFITS COME FROM?

A ship in harbor is safe—but that is not what ships are for.
                                        —John A. Shedd (1859 to circa 1928)

In seminars around the world, we have presented to participants the following factors of production in any economy, and the type of income derived therefrom:

Land = Rents

Labor = Salaries and Wages

Capital = Interest, Dividends, and Capital Gains

We then ask a deceptively simple question: Where do profits come from? The answers range from entrepreneurs and value, to revenue minus expenses, and customers. Nevertheless, the real answer is, profits come from *risk*. The word "entrepreneur" comes from the French word *entreprendre,* meaning "to undertake." It is the basis for the English word *enterprise*. But not just entrepreneurs (or feminine, entrepreneuses) make profits; so do established enterprises.

When a business engages in innovation, it is taking a risk. In Italian, the word "risk" derives from *risicare,* which means "to dare," which implies a choice, not a fate, as Peter L. Bernstein points out in his outstanding study of risk, *Against the Odds*. In other words, risk is an economic positive. There are five responses when confronted with risk: avoid it, reduce it, transfer it, accept it, or increase it. In the final analysis, a business cannot eliminate risk, as that would eliminate profits. The goal is to take calculated risks and choose them wisely. The problem in many firms is they are operating in order not to lose, rather than to win. By setting a nice comfortable floor on their earnings (via the cost-plus pricing mechanism), they have placed an artificial ceiling over their heads as well. This is self-imposed, and it comes from the attempt to avoid risk and uncertainty (which is very costly in terms of lost opportunities).

Consider labor unions, the epitome of an institution attempting to avoid risk. Talk with union members and you quickly discover they credit the union for their standard of living. Certainly, they are paid an above-market wage (Milton Friedman has proved this point) and receive good benefits, a healthy pension, and generous time off. But have you ever met a wealthy rank-and-file union member? The trade-off they made for their union compensation package is an artificial ceiling they can never rise above, at least not while employed in a union job, since seniority and other stultifying restrictions limit their potential. Risk avoidance is the antithesis to a successful enterprise, condemning it to mediocrity, perhaps even extinction. The goal should be to maximize wealth-creating opportunities rather than to minimize risk, as Peter Drucker pointed out:

> A business always saws off the limb on which it sits; it makes existing risks riskier or creates new ones. . . . Risk is of the essence, and risk making and risk taking constitute the basic function of enterprise. . . . This risk is something quite different from risk in the statistician's probability; it is risk of the unique event, the irreversible qualitative breaking of the pattern (quoted in Kehrer, 1989: 53).

Drucker is explaining a basic economic theory known as Böhm-Bawerk's law—named after the Austrian economist Eugen Böhm-Bawerk (1851–1926)—which states, "Existing means of production can yield greater economic performance only through greater uncertainty; through taking greater risk" (ibid: 298). Businesses have very sophisticated means of measuring the costs and benefits of risks, *once they have been taken*. But the risk occurs only *before* the event, and cannot be accurately measured until *after* it has occurred. There is no theory—in economics or finance—that measures the cost of *not* taking a risk. Yet it is precisely these losses that cost the business the most.

Risk and uncertainty are the twin banes of human existence. Consider what people will sacrifice to avoid them. Risk avoidance has created a $1.5 trillion worldwide insurance industry. It is why rental car companies make more from the collision damage waiver insurance they sell than they do renting cars. It is why buyers of appliances (e.g., microwaves, stereos, and other electronic goods) will spend large sums on extended warranties for products that could be replaced more cheaply. It is why criminals and prosecutors plea-bargain, each being uncertain as to what a jury is going to do (completely rational behavior).

Peter Drucker classified risk into three categories: the affordable, the nonaffordable, and the compulsory:

> First, there was the risk a business could afford to take. If it succeeded at the innovation, it would not achieve major results, and if it failed, it would not do great corporate damage. Second, there was the risk a business could not afford to take. This risk usually involved an innovation that the company lacked the knowledge to implement, and usually would end up building the competition's business. Third, there was the risk a business could not afford not to take. Failure to undertake this innovation meant there might not be a business several years hence (quoted in Flaherty, 1999: 172).

Naturally, in this book, the third type of risk taking will be advocated. That is, taking those risks that will spur the firm to higher levels of effectiveness and profitability. Too often in organizations, risk taking is seen as a negative, a reckless use of resources better spent on other functions. Nothing could be further from the truth. Committing a portion of today's resources to future expectations certainly entails risk, but since that is the source of profits—not to mention innovation, dynamism, and economic growth—it is a process inherent in the function of business entities. Economywide, profits may only constitute 10 percent of what the American economy produces, but in terms of creating an incentive to effectively produce the other

90 percent, they are essential. And profits are derived from risk; complacency is not an option.

This, by the way, is another defect you may care to note about the new equation, because it makes it look as if profitability appears by effectively leveraging intellectual capital at the right price, but misses the importance of risk. We must always remember that profits, ultimately, are derived from risk taking, and no equation, no matter how complex and intricate, will ever be able to capture the essence of an entrepreneur, an effective executive, or profit-making enterprise.

This chapter has laid the groundwork for the remaining chapters, and the remaining books in the Intellectual Capitalism Series. I have covered a lot of material here, and have presented some radical (Latin for "from the root") ideas. I have argued that the old equation is not worthy of enterprises that, more and more, are composed of knowledge workers because it leverages the wrong things and does not explain the elements of success in an intellectual capital economy. The new equation is a worthy model for the noble calling of enterprise. And while there are still shortcomings in the equation, it is a starting point for understanding the drivers of success for the business of the future.

When I first publicly presented and contrasted the new equation with the old one at a seminar for a professional service firm, an attendee explained to me at the break why she thought the new equation was so superior to the old. She said, and I'm paraphrasing here, "Your equation presents so many more factors that enable a firm to achieve its objectives than the old one did. It is like being freed from a cage that has restricted our firm for decades." It is my fervent hope this new paradigm has a similar affect on all who study it, and will change their behavior as a result. The old paradigm is indeed far too restricting, and it doesn't represent the realities of the marketplace in which companies find themselves currently. The enterprises of the future must lead the way by following a model worthy of a proud heritage of free minds operating in free markets being the catalyst for dynamism and growth.

Modern firms are knowledge organizations and it is time for them to begin acting as if they understood this fact, rather than trying to constantly enhance efficiency by treating their human capital as if they had no mind of their own, redolent of the days of Frederick Taylor's time-and-motion studies. Humans are not simply machines that exist to operate at peak efficiency, and the old equation keeps us mired in this mentality. I believe we can—indeed, must—do better than the opportunities presented by an antiquated model. Let us now continue our historical analysis on the origins of this model to discover how we arrived at where we are.

5

PANTOMETRISTS: COUNTING FOR THE SAKE OF COUNTING

*Grown-ups love figures. When you tell them that you have
made a new friend, they never ask you any questions about
essential matters. They never say to you, "What does his voice
sound like? What games does he love best? Does he collect
butterflies?" Instead they demand: "How old is he? How many
brothers has he? How much does he weigh? How much money
does his father make?" Only from these figures do they
think they have learned anything about him.*

Antoine de Saint-Exupéry, *The Little Prince,* 1943

In the sixteenth century, a new word appeared in English dictionaries—
pantometry, which means universal measurement. Ever since, man has been
obsessed with counting things, from people and sheep to the amount of cars
imported and the number of McDonald's hamburgers served. Being able to
count and measure is another one of the traits separating man from animals.
The famous quotation of Scottish mathematician and physicist Lord Kelvin
(1824–1907) is inscribed—slightly inaccurately—in the stones of the Social
Science Building at the University of Chicago:

> When you cannot measure it, when you cannot express it in numbers,
> your knowledge is of a meagre and unsatisfactory kind. . . . It may be the
> beginning of knowledge, but you have scarcely in your thoughts advanced
> to the stage of science (quoted in McCloskey, 2000: 80).

The problem for the pantometrists is the same one facing businesspeople today: what should be measured? Facts and figures do not provide
a context, or reveal truth; we still need our imaginations and creativity. Lord
Kelvin's statement cannot be expressed in numbers, but that does not automatically make it "meagre and unsatisfactory." If everything important has
to be quantified to be comprehended, how are we to understand art, music,

25

poetry, literature—indeed, our own human feelings? Indeed, one could argue the more valuable something is, the more likely it *cannot* be quantified.

Statistics can certainly pronounce a fact, but they cannot explain it without an underlying context, or theory. Numbers have an unfortunate tendency to supersede other types of knowing. The human brain is capable of assimilating literally thousands of pieces of information, from facial and body expressions, inflection, and tone of voice to experiences and intuition, to draw conclusions. This is why juries are instructed to *judge* the guilt or innocence of a defendant based on concepts such as "beyond reasonable doubt" or a "preponderance of the evidence," not to precisely *measure* their verdicts.

Numbers give the illusion of presenting more truth and precision than they are capable of providing. The alphabet contains only 26 letters, so how hard can writing be? John Stuart Mill (1806–1873), moral philosopher and author of *Principles of Political Economy*—no intellectual slouch—was tormented by the thought of a theoretical limit to the amount of music that could be composed from the seemingly limited seven notes of the music scale.

Jeremy Bentham (1748–1832), the founder of social utilitarianism, and author of *Introduction to the Principles of Morals and Legislation,* published in 1789, is famous for his theory that mankind is governed by two sovereign masters, pain and pleasure. He thought this pleasure-pain nexus needed quantification—what he termed "felicific calculus"—and he took great pains to try and measure both, with *utils,* as if one could put a numerical value on joy and sorrow. Bentham thought the ultimate goal of society should be the *greatest happiness principle*—"the greatest happiness of the greatest number." No doubt his insights led to cost-benefit analysis, which states a project should be undertaken only if the benefits outweigh the costs. Yet the bigger problem for Bentham was that numbers alone did not provide the answer as to *how* to achieve happiness for everyone.

When English economist Robert Malthus (1766–1834) predicted mass starvation in his 1798 book, *An Essay on the Principle of Population* (because population would grow at a geometric pace while food production increased only arithmetically), all the figures he looked at did not provide the solution to the alleged problem. This same number-crunching analysis led the French revolutionary Count de Mirabeau to remark: "Men will multiply up to the limits of subsistence like rats in a barn." It turned out Malthus was wrong, largely because he did nothing but analyze the numbers; he did not take into account the immeasurable ingenuity of man to solve an ever increasing range of problems.

Exhibit 5.1   Jeremy Bentham's preserved body, located at the London University.

Photo by Paul O'Byrne

Only a *statist* (which is what the first statisticians were called until as late as 1878—if you are going to count something, it must remain still) poring over tables and graphs of population data would draw the remarkable conclusion that an addition of one more human life is nothing but a drain on resources, rather than the ultimate creator of an ever abundant supply of the sustenance needed to sustain a growing population in prosperity.

Surely even Malthus understood this difference, since he fathered three children, exceeding the replacement birthrate for a nation of 2.1 children per family. Still, over several centuries, statists fastidiously collected numbers on births, deaths, and marriages, but no systematic analysis occurred until the age of the Scientific Revolution well into the seventeenth century. A cursory glance at the Bill of Mortality for London during the Great Plague of 1665 demonstrates the crudeness of the statistics collected during this time period. It listed category of deaths as follows:

Ague and Feaver	5,257
Executed	21
Teeth and worms	2,614
Frighted	23
Gout and Sciatica	27
Grief	46
Plague	68,596
Lethargy	14
Griping in the Guts	1,288

(Boyle, 2001: 48)

These categories would befuddle a modern-day actuary, as they don't provide very consistent or reliable data (how does one explain grief and lethargy?). As the Scientific Revolution progressed, man got better at counting and measuring the population, but not everyone was enamored with the idea of conducting a census. In Britain, York MP William Thornton defeated the idea of a census, by arguing:

"Can it be pretended, that by the knowledge of our number, or our wealth, either can be increased? And what purpose will it answer to know where the kingdom is crowded, and where it is thin, except we are to be driven from place to place as graziers do their cattle? If this be intended, let them brand up at once; but while they treat us like oxen and sheep, let them not insult us with the name of men (ibid: 50).

The prominent biographer, historian, social, literary, and political critic Thomas Carlyle (1795–1881) certainly concurred with Thornton's sentiments, stating: "Tables are like cobwebs . . . beautifully reticulated, orderly to look upon, but which will hold no conclusion. Tables are abstractions" (Cohen, 2005: 147).

Charles Dickens' *Hard Times,* published in 1854, is dedicated to Thomas Carlyle. In a letter to Carlyle requesting permission to dedicate his work, Dickens wrote: [*Hard Times*] is a novel concerned to "shake people in a terrible mistake of these days." This mistake: utilitarian philosophy and narrowly conceived rationality. Dickens considered these ideas a fallacious conception of human nature, which made no allowance for human qualities such as generosity, altruism, and imaginative sympathy. Their concern with quantitative analysis made them insensitive to the individual. The protagonist in the novel, Thomas Gradgrind, is obsessed with statistics and rational analysis, calling on his young students by number and instructing his daughter, "Louisa, never wonder! By means of addition, subtraction, multiplication, and division, settle everything somehow, and never wonder" (Dickens, 1998: 64).

This sterile and analytical view of the world comes across from Gradgrind when his daughter seeks his advice about a marriage proposal from his friend, Mr. Bounderby: she wants to know what she should consider if not love, to which he replies:

> "Why, my dear Louisa, I would advise you (since you ask me) to consider this question, as you have been accustomed to consider every other question, simply as one of tangible Fact. The ignorant and the giddy may embarrass such subjects with irrelevant fancies, and other absurdities that have no existence, properly viewed, really no existence — but it is no compliment to you to say, that you know better. Now, what are the Facts of this case? You are, we will say in round numbers, twenty years of age; Mr. Bounderby is, we will say in round numbers, fifty. There is some disparity in your respective years, but in your means and positions there is none; on the contrary, there is a great suitability. Then the question arises, Is this one disparity sufficient to operate as a bar to such a marriage? In considering this question, it is not unimportant to take into account the statistics of marriage, so far as they have yet been obtained, in England and Wales. I find, on reference to the figures, that a large proportion of these marriages are contracted between parties of very unequal ages, and that the elder of these contracting parties is, in rather more than three-fourths of these instances, the bride-groom."

> "Louisa, it appears to me that nothing can be plainer. Confining yourself rigidly to Fact, the question of Fact you state to yourself is: Does Mr. Bounderby ask me to marry him? Yes, he does. The sole remaining question then is: Shall I marry him? I think nothing can be plainer than that?" (ibid: 130–31).

The ultimate manifestation of the numerical mentality was Robert McNamara, President John F. Kennedy's secretary of defense from 1961 to 1968, thereafter president of the World Bank. McNamara was an accounting instructor at Harvard Business School before World War II, then served as a specialist in operations research projects with the U.S. government during the war. After the war, he was hired by Henry Ford II—along with the so-called Whiz Kids—to revitalize the sagging profits of the Ford Motor Company. He brought a mechanistic mind-set to the War in Vietnam, trying to micromanage it by the numbers. He apologized for this ill-conceived strategy in his 1995 autobiography, *In Retrospect: The Tragedy and Lessons of Vietnam.*

Blindly relying on measurements can obscure important realities. The ultimate problem with numbers and measurements is what they *don't* tell us, and how they provide a false sense of security and control—that we know everything that is going on. In fact, one could put forth the argument, running counter to the McKinsey maxim, that the most important things in life *cannot* be measured. Despite Bentham's noble attempt, how do you measure happiness? How do you measure love, joy, respect, or trust? How do you measure the success of your marriage?

Another example of how measuring income cannot only mislead but actually obscure reality is by looking at the per capita incomes of the towns of Stanford (at the California University) and East Palo Alto, California. If you were never to visit these two places and merely relied on income and wealth statistics, you would emphatically conclude that East Palo Alto is wealthier than Stanford, since most of the residents at Stanford are students, hence have relatively low incomes. If we are going to count and measure, we should do so only with those things that are *truly* meaningful.

For as much as the pantometrists counted and measured, it didn't provide them the insights required to ameliorate the problems they were enumerating. More accurate counting did not tell Malthus *how* to restrain the population any more than it instructed Bentham *how* to make people happier. One still needed to use imagination, creativity, and judgment to interpret the numbers' meaning; but a constant diet of facts and figures provides us with a false sense of knowing, crowding out the more essential insights, which only come from human intuition.

This lack of imagination and faith in the future even affected Lord Kelvin, who dismissed radio as pointless, heavier-than-air flying machines as impossible, X-rays as a hoax, and stated to an assemblage of physicists at the British Association for the Advancement of Science in 1900: "There is nothing new to be discovered in physics now. All that remains is more and more precise measurement." As Albert Einstein said: "Sometimes what counts can't be counted, and what can be counted doesn't count."

A measurement without a theory is merely a fact, and there is nothing as useless as a fact not illuminated by a theory; we may as well read the phone book. A physicist may be able to calculate the velocity of two billiard balls hurtling toward each other and predict when they will collide. But what if two human beings are racing toward each other and we are limited to merely quantitative analysis, leaving out more important subjective evidence such as: Are they friends or foes? Happy, mad, or sad? Until we knew the answers to these questions, we would not be able to predict an outcome.

Human action tends to be what economists call *purposeful behavior.* It is free will put into operation. In contrast, a billiard ball moves because it is hit by another; it can't decide for itself. A physicist cannot explain why a car goes to Wal-Mart rather than Kmart. Human beings do not lend themselves to easy measurements.

Perhaps we need a corollary to the McKinsey maxim: What is really important cannot be measured. This is what author David Boyle calls the "McKinsey Fallacy." Yet this will no doubt be met with tremendous resistance. It goes against the very grain of the MBA mind-set, the modern-day pantometrists, who are taught everything needs to be quantified and counted, and decisions should be based on the numbers. In other words, don't think, count.

The Russian novelist and social critic Alexander Solzhenitsyn once said, "It is a very dangerous thing to speak against the fashion of the times." But I am going to do it anyway, and I begin by reviewing how the McKinsey maxim became the conventional wisdom by looking at the origins of the Scientific Management Revolution.

6

THE GOSPEL OF EFFICIENCY

Why is it that when I buy a pair of hands, I always
get a human being as well?

—Henry Ford

To symbolize his nationalist objectives, Mohandas Gandhi proposed an Indian flag with a 24-spoked blue *chakra* (wheel) in the center, representing economic self-sufficiency. Gandhi was certainly an inspiring leader, but he was a dreadful economist. A jack-of-all-trades would lead a poor, nasty, brutal, and short life. Not only would he remain impecunious by attempting complete economic self-sufficiency—what economists call *autarky*—so would an entire country.

One innovative economics instructor assigns his students the class project of attempting to make for themselves products they naturally take for granted and normally purchase, such as clothing, beer, electronic equipment,

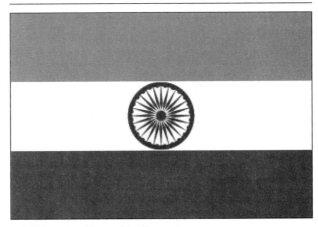

Exhibit 6.1   Flag of India.

and so forth. There is no quicker method to illustrate how difficult life would be if we relied on self-sufficiency. Very few people would become wealthy. The moral is, do what you do best and trade for the rest.

This was, essentially, Adam Smith's starting point in his book, *An Inquiry into the Nature and Causes of the Wealth of Nations.* Smith wanted to explain why some countries were wealthy, not why most countries were poor (notice the title wasn't *An Inquiry into the Nature and Causes of the Poverty of Nations*). Poverty needs no explanation, nor do we learn much from studying it; it is the natural condition of man since he emerged from the cave. What would we do once we discovered the *root causes* of poverty? Create more of it? What needs to be explained is wealth, not poverty, since the most effective antidote to poverty is wealth.

Smith posited that the welfare of a nation depended on its production, and the amount of production depended upon the division and specialization of labor. Specialization of labor is the idea of people or nations producing a narrower range of goods and services than they consume, which is why modern economies are dependent on a far wider range of people to provide for their daily sustenance. The division of labor breaks down a production process into many small steps and performs those steps separately, with different workers doing different tasks, as on an assembly line. While specialization makes us productive, division of labor is what makes us rich.

Despite present-day management gurus who claim to have discovered the concept of core competency, in reality this is a very old principle, which Smith explicated in his book, in the famous example of the operation of a pin factory:

> One man draws out the wire, another straightens it, a third cuts it, a fourth points it, a fifth grinds it at the top for receiving the head; to make the head requires two or three distinct operations; to put it on is a peculiar business; to whiten it is another; it is even a trade by itself to put them into paper. . . . I have seen a small manufactory of this kind where ten men only were employed and where some of them performed two or three distinct operations. But though they were very poor, and therefore but indifferently accommodated with the necessary machinery, they could, when they exerted themselves, make among them about twelve pounds of pins a day. There are in a pound upwards of four thousand pins of a middling size. Those ten persons, therefore, could make among them upwards of forty-eight thousand pins in a day. . . . But if they had all wrought separately and independently . . . they certainly could not each of them make twenty . . . perhaps not one pin a day (quoted in Dougherty, 2002: 53).

Exhibit 6.2   The gravesite of Adam Smith (1723–1790), Edinburgh, Scotland. "I love your company, gentlemen, but I believe I must leave you to go to another world." (Smith's last words to his friends).

Photo by Paul O'Byrne

Smith's pin factory illustrates the importance of the *division and specialization of labor,* a central cause of the wealth of nations Smith so eloquently wrote about.

Similar to Smith's tour of the pin factory, Henry Ford had a similar epiphany when touring a Chicago meatpacking plant, where he saw animal carcasses hung on an overhead rail being moved from butcher to butcher. When Ford inquired how long they had been processing meat like this, the reply was something to the effect that, "This is how we have done it for years." Hence a tradition in one industry became a quantum revolution in another.

Even though Adam Smith wrote about the specialization and division of labor in the 1770s—when the Industrial Revolution was in its infancy— it would be another 100 years before another revolution would take place to increase dramatically the productivity of factory workers throughout the world, largely from the efforts of one man with a stopwatch.

THE SCIENTIFIC MANAGEMENT REVOLUTION

The most famous preacher of the efficiency gospel was Frederick Winslow Taylor, who observed endless ways to make laborers' work more rational, quantifiable, and scientific, writing about the "science of shoveling" and the "law of heavy laboring," topics that today would most likely make for lack-luster book sales, but in Taylor's time ushered in a new era of management thinking. Taylor was born on March 20, 1856, into a prominent Quaker family in an upper-middle-class suburb of Philadelphia. As a teenager he became obsessed with cricket, which, like baseball, is a game where the statistics and batting averages are more exciting than the game itself. Allegedly, he never smoked or drank alcohol, tea, or coffee. And when he went to dances, he drew up charts classifying all the girls in attendance as attractive or ugly and precisely calculated his time so he spent one-half in conversation with each.

Exhibit 6.3 Frederick Winslow Taylor (1856–1915).

Taylor became an industrial engineer, testing his time-and-motion theories on the factory floor among his coworkers at the Midvale Steel Company in Philadelphia. As David Boyle explains in his wonderful book, *The Sum of Our Discontent: Why Numbers Make Us Irrational,* Taylor's experiments went something like this:

First, you break down any job into its component parts—as far as it would go, to the basic movements.

Next, you time each of those parts with a stopwatch to find out just how quickly they can be achieved by the quickest and most efficient workers.

Next, you get rid of any parts of the job that aren't necessary.

Then you add in about 40 percent to the time for unavoidable delays and rest. This bit was what he used to call "rule of thumb" before the idea of scientific management required that there be no such thing. It was always one of the most controversial parts of the package . . .

Finally, you organize your pay system so that the most efficient people can earn considerably more money by meeting the optimum times, while the average have to struggle to keep up (Boyle, 2001: 93).

Taylor took all the romance out of work, and instead of a "noble skill" it was subdivided into a series of simple motions, much as the pin workers Adam Smith observed. All of the other aspects of human beings— creativity, initiative, imagination—were to be done somewhere else in the organization, usually the province of upper management, who did the "thinking" while the workers did the "doing." This did not foster an environment of trustworthiness in the factories where Taylor's ideas were implemented, but it did yield increased productivity, which also increased the wages of the common worker. It was Taylor, after all, who replaced the phrase "working harder" with "working smarter."

Taylor's ideas were not implemented without friction, however. He viewed both managers and workers as "dumb oxen," and trade union opposition was on the increase. In 1915, Congress passed legislation, which stayed on the books until 1949, banning Taylor's beloved stopwatches from government factories.

Peter Drucker credits Taylor with coining the terms *management* and *consultant* (Taylor's calling card identified him as a "Consultant to Management," and he charged the princely sum of $35 a day—approximately $645 today—for his standard two-hour lecture), and for being the world's very first "knowledge worker." In his lecture, Taylor said every worker must ask two questions:

Every day, year in and year out, each man should ask himself over and over again, two questions. First, "What is the name of the man I am now working for?" And having answered this definitely, then, "What does this man want me to do, right now?" Not [Boyle asks], "What ought I to do in the interests of the company I am working for?" Not, "What are the duties of the position I am filling?" Not, "What did I agree to do when I came here?" Not, "What should I do for my own best interest?" but plainly and simply, "What does this man want me to do?" (ibid: 94).

Even Russian communist leader Vladimir Ilych Lenin came under Taylor's spell: "We must introduce in Russia the study and teaching of the new Taylor System and its systematic trial and adaptation" (quoted in Skousen, 2001: 252). On the eve of the Bolshevik Revolution, Lenin declared that "accounting and control" were the key factors in running an enterprise and that capitalism had already "reduced" management to "extraordinarily simple operations" that "any literate person can perform"—that is, "supervising and recording, knowledge of the four rules of arithmetic, and issuing appropriate receipts." Such "exceedingly simple operations of registration, filing and checking" could, according to Lenin, "easily be performed" by people receiving ordinary workmen's wages (from Lenin's *The State and Revolution,* quoted in Sowell, 2000: 111).

Taylor wrote all of his theories down throughout the years, circulating them privately in 1911 in *The Principles of Scientific Management.* Taylor's theories have been credited with tripling output during World War II and making Mussolini's trains run on time in Italy; German precision engineering, Lenin's Five-Year Plans, consumerism, Hitler's gas chambers, and the death of communism, all with a simple stopwatch. No doubt Taylor contributed to most of these, some more than others, earning him the nickname "Speedy Taylor."

Some of Taylor's principles set forth in *The Principles of Scientific Management* are worth noting to compare them to what is needed to increase the effectiveness of today's knowledge workers (to be discussed in Chapter 12):

> In the past the man has been first; in the future the system must be first (Taylor, 1967: 7).

> . . . [T]he workman who is best suited to actually doing the work is incapable of fully understanding this science, without the guidance and help of those who are working with him or over him, either through lack of education or through insufficient mental capacity (ibid: 26).

> . . . [A]lmost every act of the workman should be preceded by one or more preparatory acts of the management which enable him to do his work better and quicker than he otherwise could (ibid: 26).

> Perhaps the most prominent single element in modern scientific management is the task idea. The work of every workman is fully planned out by the management at least one day in advance, and each man receives in most cases complete written instructions, describing in detail the task which he is to accomplish, as well as the means to be used in doing the work (ibid: 39).

> The first illustration is that of handling pig iron. This work is so crude and elementary in its nature that the writer firmly believes that it would

be possible to train an intelligent gorilla so as to become a more efficient pig-iron handler than any man can be (ibid: 40).

> The average boy would go very slowly if, instead of being given a task, he were told to do as much as he could. All of us are grown-up children, and it is equally true that the average workman will work with the greatest satisfaction, both to himself and to his employer, when he is given each day a definite task which he is to perform in a given time, and which constitutes a proper day's work for a good workman. This furnishes the workman with a clear-cut standard, by which he can throughout the day measure his own progress, and the accomplishment of which affords him the greatest satisfaction (ibid: 120–21).

This advice seems crude and unenlightened in today's knowledge economy, and organized labor viewed Taylorism as nothing more than a method to extract more sweat from labor, turning workers into impersonal slaves. One worker describe it thusly: "Scientific management was degrading. . . . In standing over you with a stopwatch, peering at you, measuring you, rating you, it treated you like a side of beef. You weren't supposed to think. Whatever workmanly pride you might once have possessed must be sacrificed on the altar of efficiency" (quoted in Skousen, 2001: 252–53).

Henry Ford wrote in his autobiography *My Life and Work*: "Factory organization is not a device to prevent the expansion of ability, but a device to reduce the waste and losses due to mediocrity. It is not a device to hinder the ambitious, clear-headed man from doing his best, but a device to prevent the don't-care sort of individual from doing his worst" (Ford, 1922: 270). Not exactly an enlightened view of industrial organization, but it is also difficult to argue with Ford's ability to put the automobile within reach of the common man. There is no doubt that we owe a large portion of our present standard of living to Taylor and his methods of increasing the productivity of manual workers.

Yet Taylor certainly did not view his methods as a way to extract more labor from each worker. One must consider how truly revolutionary these ideas were in Taylor's day, and his motivation for proposing them. His objective was not cost reduction, but rather to increase productivity to benefit the worker, not the owner, enabling capital and labor to enjoy a harmonious relationship. In fact, Taylor considered himself to be the "Great Harmonizer." He was one of the first to recognize the need to apply knowledge to work, even though he may have believed this to be the task primarily of management rather than the workers themselves. He agreed with Adam Smith's vision of universal opulence, and wrote: "the luxuries of one generation [will become] the necessities of the next [and] the working people of our country will live as well and have the same luxuries, the same opportunities for leisure, for culture, and for education, as are now possessed by the average business man" (quoted in Skousen, 2001: 253).

Not only would an increase in productivity be good for owners and workers, it would be a positive boon for customers as well. Andrew Carnegie ruthlessly focused on output per man-hour and unit costs, in order to slash prices, arguing that since steel was essential for a modern economy, reducing its price would lower the prices of virtually everything, thereby raising living standards. Carnegie was able to get the price of steel rails, which cost $160 a ton in 1875, down to $17 a ton by 1898, all the while paying his managers the highest wages in U.S. industry.

Exhibit 6.4
Frank Gilbreth
(1868–1924).

In 1907, Taylor met a bricklayer, Frank Gilbreth, who had done his own time-and-motion analysis on laying bricks, and was able to increase his output from 1,000 to 2,700 per day. Apparently, Gilbreth was more obsessed with his stopwatch than was Taylor, and 2 of his 12 children later wrote a portrait of him titled *Cheaper by the Dozen,* later made into a Hollywood movie with Clifton Webb as Gilbreth. If Taylor was idiosyncratic, Gilbreth was an even stranger duck, as David Boyle humorously points out:

Gilbreth was obsessed with measuring, breaking down every manual operation into what he called "therbligs" (Gilbreth spelled backward). He buttoned his vest from the bottom up because it took four seconds less than buttoning it from the top down. He cut 17 seconds off his shaving time by using two brushes. Using two shavers cut 44 seconds, but then he cut himself and had to spend another two minutes looking for a plaster. He took most of his children with him on business trips and around factories, armed with pens and pads, but their home in Montclair, New Jersey, sounded a bit like Taylor's factories:

[According to one of Gilbreth's children] "Dad installed process and work charts in the bathrooms. Every child old enough to write—and Dad expected his offspring to start writing at a tender age—was required to initial the chart in the morning, after he had brushed his teeth, taken a bath, combed his hair, and made his bed. At night each child had to weigh himself, plot the figure on a graph and initial the process charts again after he had done his homework, washed his hands and face, and brushed his teeth. Mother wanted to have a place on the chart for saying prayers, but Dad said as far as he was concerned, prayers were voluntary (Boyle, 2001: 100).

Why this relentless focus on saving time? Because, as Benjamin Franklin wrote in 1748, and what has since become the conventional wisdom of commerce . . .

TIME IS MONEY

This now-familiar adage has certainly infected the way businesspeople view the value of the products and services they offer. Unfortunately, it is taken out of context. Franklin wrote the famous words in a letter to a young businessperson just starting out, who had sought Franklin's advice. Here is what Franklin wrote, in its entirety, on the subject of time in the letter, entitled "Advice to a Young Tradesman":

> To my friend, A.B.:
>
> As you have desired it of me, I write the following hints, which have been of service to me, and may, if observed, be so to you. Remember that time is money. He that can earn ten shillings a day by his labor, and goes abroad, or sits idle, one half of that day, though he spends but sixpence during his diversion or idleness, ought not to reckon that the only expense; he has really spent, or rather thrown away, five shillings besides (quoted in Krass, 1999: 283).

Note that Franklin was not speaking of value, nor price; he was articulating the concept of opportunity cost. This is the idea (coined by the Austrian economist Friedrich von Wieser [1851–1926]) that every activity or product in the economy has an alternative use. It is an important economic principle, but a seller's opportunity cost has little to do with value provided to the customer, or the productivity of workers (this is explained in greater depth in the first book of the Intellectual Capitalism Series, *Pricing on Purpose: Creating and Capturing Value*). Yet throughout history, humans have always correlated labor with value, inputs with outputs. In medieval English, the word "acre" represented the amount of land a team of eight oxen could plow in a morning. Even Thomas Jefferson used time-and-motion analysis — before Frederick Taylor was born — to investigate whether a wheelbarrow with two wheels was more efficient than with one.

According to anthropologists, you can tell a lot about a culture by the way it views time, what they call the "silent language." The pace of our lives determines our views about the passage of time. J. T. Fraser, the founder of the International Society for the Study of Time, summed it up well: "Tell me what to think of time, and I shall know what to think of you" (quoted in Levine, 1997: xv, xix).

In his fascinating book, *A Geography of Time,* Robert Levine points out that before the first mechanical clocks had been invented, the idea of coordinating people's activities was almost impossible. Appointments usually took place at dawn. "It is no coincidence that, historically, so many important events occurred at sunrise—duels, battles, meetings" (ibid: 60).

The first known mechanical timepieces appeared in Europe in the fourteenth century. These clocks had a specific purpose: "to inform pious monks when it was time to pray" (ibid: 56). Throughout history, clocks have come progressively closer to the person. We have progressed from the public clocks of the Middle Ages to clocks inside the home to pocket watches to those attached to our bodies. The wristwatch appeared around 1850 (referred by some as "the handcuff of our time"). In fact, some would argue that it is the clock, not the steam engine, that is the key machine of the Industrial Age. Active economies all over the world place great emphasis on time, and economics certainly drives the pace and tempo of modern life.

In an 1891 brochure for the Electric Signal Clock Company, the time clock named the Autocrat was featured, touting these benefits:

> Gives military precision, and teaches practicality, promptness and precision wherever adopted. A school, office or factory installing this system is not at the caprice of a forgetful bell ringer, nor anyone's watch, as the office clock is now the standard time for the plant," [providing management and supervisors a means to extend their disciplinary reach beyond their vision].
>
> The 1914 catalog of the International Time Recording Company [later to become IBM] suggested that time clocks would "save money, enforce discipline and add to the productive time." Also, the time recorded induces punctuality by impressing the value of time on each individual (ibid: 67–68).

Even though many workplaces no longer have time clocks for purposes of direct supervision or discipline, the mentality lives on that time is a natural way to measure the ratio of inputs and outputs, and is one of the reasons professionals—such as accountants, lawyers, advertising agencies and the like—to this day maintain timesheets. Though it should be noted that timesheets were introduced into the professions in the 1940s as a way to perform *cost accounting,* not as a tool to increase productivity.

Frank Gilbreth eventually went on to repudiate the validity of time-and-motion studies as unethical and "absolutely worthless." In the meantime, Taylor pressed on, espousing his theories until his final day. In the winter of 1914, hospitalized with pneumonia, every morning Taylor arose out of bed to wind his precious watch. One morning, March 21, 1915, a nurse saw

Exhibit 6.5   The astronomical clock in Prague was originally constructed in 1410.

Photo by Paul O'Byrne

him winding it uncharacteristically early, 4:30 A.M. When she returned a half hour later, Taylor was dead; it was one day after his fifty-ninth birthday. Many of the so-called efficiency experts met an early death—which makes you wonder what, exactly, were they saving all that time for?

From the latter part of the nineteenth century to the Great Depression, as schools and businesses were installing time clocks and conducting time-and-motion studies, to implement Taylorism, the Progressive Era was also ushering in another wave of growth for scientific management, marked by expanding governmental regulation of the economy. The adoption of the income tax, creation of the Federal Trade Commission and Federal Reserve Bank, along with the Securities Act of 1933 and the Securities Exchange Act of 1934, created the demand for more efficiency and greater accuracy in macroeconomic data, leading to the advent of national income statistics.

During the 1920s, when economists began to recognize a large and growing sector of the labor force known as *service workers,* they used metrics similar to Taylor's to measure their productivity—from the number of transactions a bank teller processed and tables a waiter or waitress turned in a shift to the number of cases closed by an insurance claims adjuster.

Once man begins to measure something, the next logical step is to begin to predict it; but to do that we have to move beyond just counting and measuring, and into the world of positing and testing theories. The economics profession is well equipped to perform this role. Let us now take another important historical detour and explore how the moral philosophers of Adam Smith's day began to posit theories in order to understand human behavior and the relevance it has for all businesspeople today.

7

ALL LEARNING STARTS
WITH THEORY

It is theory which decides what we can observe.

—Albert Einstein

We are ruled by our theories, whether we are consciously aware of them or not. Theories allow us to make sense of the world around us, guide our interpretations, formulate predictions about the future, explain human behavior, and even control actions. Harvard Business School Professor Clayton Christensen has pointed out that Adam and Eve were perhaps the only researchers who started at the very bottom of the theory-building process. Mankind has been developing better theories ever since.

Praxeology, the study of human action, is a bigger challenge than analyzing the physical or biological sciences. People act purposefully, have values, make choices and mistakes, learn from the past, and are influenced by their beliefs about the eventual consequences of their actions. The behavior of animals, or inert matter, is comparatively far more predictable and not subject to the perception of the players. An astronomer can predict the cycles of the moon and tell you exactly when the sun will rise, but can you predict with any confidence when your teenager will get out of bed in the morning? With the right incentives, it may be possible to predict—or sometimes, even control—this very behavior, which is why economists persist in assuming that human beings act, for the most part, rationally.

For instance, why do businesses engage in 99-cent pricing, forcing us to give and take those useless pennies? The common answer is, "It's a sales gimmick. The customer perceives $9.99 being cheaper than $10.00." From an economic point of view, this contradicts the theory of rationality, since it implies customers, over the long run, are too ignorant to tell the difference between $9.99 and $10.00. Might there be a better explanation? In other words, how does 99-cent pricing serve someone's interests? Is it purposeful behavior based on learning from the past? Here is how economist Steven Landsburg explained the origin of 99-cent pricing, in his book *The Armchair Economist: Economics and Everyday Life*:

> The phenomenon of "99-cent pricing" seems to have first become common in the nineteenth century, shortly after the invention of the cash register. The cash register was a remarkable innovation; not only did it do simple arithmetic, it also kept a record of every sale. That's important if you think your employees might be stealing from you. You can examine the tape at the end of the day and know how much money should be in the drawer.
>
> There is one small problem with cash registers: They don't actually record every sale; they record only those sales that are rung up. If a customer buys an item for $1 and hands the clerk a dollar bill, the clerk can neglect to record the sale, slip the bill in his pocket, and leave no one the wiser.
>
> On the other hand, when a customer buys an item for 99 cents and hands the clerk a dollar bill, the clerk has to make change. This requires him to open the cash drawer, which he cannot do without ringing up the sale. Ninety-nine-cent pricing forces clerks to ring up sales and keeps them honest (Landsburg, 1993: 15–16).

Upon reflection, this appears a more adequate explanation than "sales gimmick," does it not? And it comports with the history of both the cash register and 99-cent pricing. The brothers John and James Rittney patented the cash register in 1879, even labeling it the "Incorruptible Cashier." In 1887, 5,400 cash registers were in operation, growing to 16,395 by 1890. The loud bells were installed so shopkeepers—who spent a lot of time in the backroom doing inventory and bookkeeping—could keep mental track of the number of times the drawer was opened.

One can witness this today in many retail and fast food chains, where signs are posted next to the cash register reading, "If you don't receive a receipt, your meal is free." Do the owners do this because they are concerned with the fastidiousness of your personal record keeping? Or, more rationally, are they providing you with an incentive to monitor their employees, a very low-cost way for them to keep their people honest?

This is why being grounded in a theory can be incalculably useful for understanding human behavior, which is why economists have stubbornly clung to this theory of rationality—they find it immensely valuable in explaining so much behavior. Yet this theory has been challenged by many social scientists, including economists.

These critics claim the assumption turns the average person into a cold, calculating individual whose only interest is to maximize his wealth (or utility, or power, or whatever else the person may be seeking). Why did the chicken cross the road? To maximize its utility, say the rationalists. However, what if we witness a person drinking a quart of oil and then dying? Can we really explain his behavior as rational, or that he really enjoys motor oil? Opponents of rationality point out that a theory that purports to explain everything ends up explaining nothing. They cite many examples where individuals do not appear to be behaving very rationally:

- We pay higher prices for goods and services endorsed by celebrities.
- We routinely vote in elections, even risking life and limb in inclement weather to get to the polls—even when we know our one vote won't decide the outcome.
- We leave tips in restaurants to strangers, in locations we will never visit again.
- People walk away from profitable transactions because they believe the terms are unfair.
- People have children, donate blood, return pesticides, recycle, help strangers in distress, and die wealthy, none of which appears to be "rational."
- I spoke at a conference in California once when the lottery was up to $30 million. I offered to buy a ticket—for up to 50 times the purchase price—from anyone. No one would sell to me.

Given this list, it seems as if the assumption of rationality is false, or at the least can be shown to be false in many circumstances. But rather than discard this theory, here is how Landsburg explains its usefulness:

> But the fact of the matter is that all assumptions made in all sciences are clearly false. Physicists, the most successful of scientists, routinely assume that the table is frictionless when called upon to model the motions of billiard balls. They assume that the billiard balls themselves are solid objects. They assume that objects fall in vacuums.
>
> All scientists make simplifying assumptions about the world, because the world itself is too complicated to study. All such assumptions are equally false, but not all such assumptions are equally valuable. Certain kinds of assumptions lead consistently to results that are interesting, non-obvious, and at some level testable and verifiable.
>
> The first physicist to have observed a helium-filled balloon would have admitted that there was no gravity, and the true physics of the situation

would not have been discovered. By attempting to fit unfamiliar phenomena into familiar patterns, we arrive at deeper understandings of both the patterns and the phenomena.

To a large extent, the assumption of rationality is nothing more than a commitment to inquire sympathetically into people's motives. [When we observe what at first appears to be irrational behavior] we have a choice. Either we can remark—wistfully or cynically, according to our temperament—on the inadequacy of human nature, or we can ask, "How might such behavior be serving someone's purposes?" The first option offers the satisfaction of exempting oneself from the great mass of human folly. The second offers an opportunity to learn something.

Adopting the rationality assumption means pledging to treat all human behavior as worthy of respectful consideration. In the process, we discover possibilities and develop insights that would never arise if we allowed ourselves to simply dismiss as "irrational" anything we failed to understand immediately. By disallowing the easy way out, we commit ourselves to careful and creative analysis of why people behave as they do, which is an excellent habit for any social scientist to cultivate (Landsburg, 2002: 662).

David Friedman (the son of Milton and Rose Friedman), and an outstanding economist, in his book *Hidden Order,* explains the assumption of rationality this way:

> . . . [T]he assumption describes our actions, not our thoughts. If you had to understand something intellectually in order to do it, none of us would be able to walk.
>
> Economics is based on the assumption that people have reasonably simple objectives and choose the correct means to achieve them. Both assumptions are false—but useful.
>
> Suppose someone is rational only half the time. Since there is generally one right way of doing things and many wrong ways, the rational behavior can be predicted but the irrational cannot. If we assume he is rational, we predict his behavior correctly about half the time—far from perfect, but a lot better than nothing. If I could do that well at the racetrack I would be a very rich man.
>
> . . . [R]ationality is an assumption I make about other people. I know myself well enough to allow for the consequences of my own irrationality. But for the vast mass of my fellow humans, about whom I know very little, rationality is the best predictive assumption available (Friedman, 1996: 3–5).

It is true that we can put a man on the moon yet still have people sleeping in the streets. Yet NASA has it easy, because rockets are governed by the unchanging laws of physics. Human beings are more complex; an alcoholic does not act in a manner as predicable as a rocket in orbit. The economist's theory of rationality is incredibly powerful, and explains much human behavior. After all, for all of its faults, if one is going to make a case that people consistently behave in ways that are detrimental to their own interests, the alternative better be a very convincing explanation. Otherwise, it would appear to be irrational to assume that people in general behave irrationally.

Other economic theories, such as diminishing marginal utility, allow us to explain other aspects of human behavior not normally associated with the field of economics, such as why newspaper racks do not have elaborate antitheft protections that ensure customers extract only one newspaper at a time, similar to vending machines for soda or candy. Can one conclude from this observation that buyers of the *New York Times* are more honest than the buyers of Coke, as a sociologist or criminologist might reason? Economists would answer no, that it is because the marginal value of a second, third, or fourth newspaper is not as valuable as the next Coke, which can be saved and enjoyed later.

WHY THEORIES ARE ESSENTIAL TO HUMAN PROGRESS

The sciences progress through dissension, not agreement. Theories have to be constantly tested and subjected to the principle of falsifiability, otherwise they are not scientific, merely assertions.

The concepts of hypothesis, falsification, parsimony, and the experimental method are all components of the scientific method, one of the fourteen metainventions Charles Murray documents in his fascinating and scholarly book, *Human Accomplishment* (other metainventions include: drama, the novel, logic, ethics, and Arabic numerals). Murray claims the scientific method has given us the world we inhabit today, and he dates its creation from 1589, with the publication of Galileo's *De Motu,* to 1687, with the publication of Newton's *Principia.* But he also points out that he could date the invention to 1200, and then writes: "That the basic ideas were in the air for so long without being developed suggests how complex and mind-stretching the change was" (Murray, 2003: 237).

Mind-stretching indeed. The diffusion of a new theory or idea is the process whereby an innovation is communicated through certain channels over time among the members of a social system. The term "diffusion" originates from chemistry to explain, for example, how purple iodine placed in a glass of water will diffuse until the water is lavender. It is essentially a social process, and often takes a substantial amount of time before an idea becomes accepted by an overwhelming majority of a population. When one studies the history of diffusing new ideas into a population, the timeline can stretch from decades to centuries, contrasted with the diffusion of new technology—say, for instance, going from dial-up to broadband, or the next-generation computer chip—which usually takes only a few years to reach a critical mass, or tipping point, to use the title of Malcolm Gladwell's best-selling book.

Consider, as evidence, germ theory, the idea that diseases are transmitted by specific germs, or microorganisms, as has been proved for many infectious diseases. Scholars have traced this theory back to the sixteenth century, when it was generally ignored until Jacob Henle revived it in 1840. At least since 1847, we know that the German-Hungarian physician Ignaz Philipp Semmelweis (who discovered the cause of puerperal ["childbed"] fever and introduced antisepsis into medical practice) insisted medical students at the Vienna General Hospital wash their hands between performing autopsies and examining pregnant women. (Semmelweis was later commemorated on an Austrian postage stamp.) Still, it remained on the fringes of medical science, and was not accepted by Florence Nightingale, who believed diseases were spontaneously generated from dirty or unventilated rooms and hospital wards. Not until 1865 did germ theory reach a critical mass of acceptance, becoming conventional wisdom by 1914. It is one of the most significant theories that bettered the human condition. Prior to its acceptance—until the 1920s, in fact—a trip to the doctor, on average, didn't do much good, and sometimes did a net harm.

Contemplate the fax machine, invented in 1843 by Alexander Bain, a Scottish clockmaker who called it a recording telegraph. In 1948, RCA introduced a fax machine that transmitted messages via radio waves, yet the fax machine did not diffuse into the general population until 1987—150 years to become an "overnight" success. History, science, economics, and other books are filled with similar stories.

Despite being over 400 years old, the scientific method has not been widely used by business thinkers or writers. In an overwhelming majority of business books, presentations, and advice, one of the first things you hear is, "This is not ivory tower theory, but practical steps you can take back to your office on Monday morning." I always recoil when I read books by authors who have a disdain for theory, because it usually means I am about to have my time wasted and no serious education will ensue.

This is one of the most glaring weaknesses in most business books and management ideas: they are all practice with no theory. Most do little else than propound platitudes and compose common sense into endless checklists and seven-step programs. The management consultant industry is replete with jargon, and a lot of it is even copyrighted, since legally one cannot copyright an idea. Any theory worth having can be used by others in the marketplace of ideas with impunity, so the consultants are left to protect their own verbiage. Yet there is nothing as sterile as a fact not illuminated by a theory; we may as well read the telephone book. This may explain why four out of five business books are never read to completion. Former management consultant Martin Kihn is even more critical:

> Business books are boring. They are bloated compendiums of half-baked ideas committed in fourth grade prose. Their purpose is to transform a commonsense concept or two into a consulting career through the catalyst of hollow jargon (Kihn, 2005: 17).

The schism between management theory and the scientific method is profound, one reason being the latter is relatively young compared to its older siblings in the hard sciences, which date back hundreds of years. In their piercing book *The Witch Doctors: What Management Gurus Are Saying and Why It Matters,* John Micklethwait and Adrian Wooldridge, two staff editors for *The Economist,* level this charge against the immature discipline of management theory:

> Management theory, according to the case against it, has four defects: it is constitutionally incapable of self-criticism; its terminology usually confuses rather than educates; it rarely rises above basic common sense; and it is faddish and bedeviled by contradictions that would not be allowed in more rigorous disciplines. The implication of all four charges is that management gurus are con artists, the witch doctors of our age, playing on business people's anxieties in order to sell snake oil. The gurus, many of whom have sprung suspiciously from the "great university of life" rather than any orthodox academic discipline, exist largely because people let them get away with it. Modern management theory is no more reliable than tribal medicine. Witch doctors, after all, often got it right—by luck, by instinct, or by trial and error (Micklethwait and Wooldridge, 1996: 12).

All theories are subject to falsification, precisely how all science progresses. This is an interesting phenomenon, because it implies most new theories—and especially management fads of the month—have to be wrong or irrelevant or else knowledge would proceed at lightning speed and advance by Newtonian or Einsteinian leaps every day. It does not. This makes it difficult for editors and publishers to admit most of what they publish is trivial, or just plain incorrect. In reality, knowledge progresses slowly, in a never-ending iterative process best characterized as *knowledge creep.* Fortunately, this schism is starting to narrow in the field of management research, as we shall see next.

8

CONSTRUCTING A THEORY

The only way to look into the future is use theories since conclusive data is only available about the past.

—Clayton Christensen, et al., *Seeing What's Next: Using the Theories of Innovation to Predict Industry Change,* 2004

The seminal management thinker Peter Drucker (1909–2005) certainly understood the difference between counting and theory. His writings on management span over half a century and his observations were nearly always grounded in the scientific method of observation, hypotheses, and falsification. One of his many articles published in the *Harvard Business Review* (September–October 1994) was entitled "The Theory of the Business," which laid out what he considered to be the essential elements executives would have to define in order to create wealth. It is worth quoting from at length to help you begin the process of positing better theories in your organization:

> Not in a very long time—not, perhaps, since the late 1940s or early 1950s—have there been as many new major management techniques as there are today: downsizing, outsourcing, total quality management, economic value analysis, benchmarking, reengineering. Each is a powerful tool. But, with the exceptions of outsourcing and reengineering, these tools are designed primarily to do differently what is already being done. They are "how to do" tools.
>
> Yet "what to do" is increasingly becoming the central challenge facing managements, especially those of big companies that have enjoyed long-term success (Drucker, 2003: 3).
>
> What accounts for this apparent paradox? The assumptions on which the organization has been built and is being run no longer fit reality. These are the assumptions that shape any organization's behavior, dictate its decisions about what to do and what not to do, and define what the organization considers meaningful results. These assumptions are about

markets. They are about identifying customers and competitors, their values and behavior. They are about technology and its dynamics, about a company's strengths and weaknesses. These assumptions are about what a company gets paid for. They are what I call a company's *theory of the business* (ibid: 3–4).

In fact, what underlies the current malaise of so many large and successful organizations worldwide is that their theory of the business no longer works (ibid: 4).

It usually takes years of hard work, thinking, and experimenting to reach a clear, consistent, and valid theory of the business. Yet to be successful, every organization must work one out.

What are the specifications of a valid theory of the business? There are four:

1. *The assumptions about environment, mission, and core competencies must fit reality.*
2. *The assumptions in all three areas have to fit one another.*
3. *The theory of the business must be known and understood throughout the organization.*
4. *The theory of the business has to be tested constantly.* It is not graven on tablets of stone. It is a hypothesis. And so, built into the theory of the business must be the ability to change itself (ibid: 10–11).

Even if a particular business did not follow Drucker's sage advice and postulate a theory of its business, one could certainly argue that since the macroeconomic environment of nearly any developed country is comprised of millions of businesses, the aggregate marketplace is a testable hypothesis in its own right, whereby customers spending their own money ultimately falsify the theory of any one particular firm.

All ideas and theories are, ultimately, subjected to this authentication process. In his influential book on knowledge, *Knowledge and Decisions,* Thomas Sowell delineates various kinds of ideas by their relationship to this authentication process: "There are ideas systematically prepared for authentication ('theories'), ideas not derived from any systematic process ('visions'), ideas which could not survive any reasonable authentication process ('illusions'), ideas which exempt themselves from any authentication process ('myths'), ideas which have already passed authentication processes ('facts'), as well as ideas known to have failed—or certain to fail—such processes ('falsehoods'—both mistakes and lies)" (Sowell, 1980: 4–5).

In a business enterprise, economists say two sources of profit are possible: an *economic* profit and an *epistemological* profit, the latter of which has the capability to advance specific knowledge. The market, meaning the sovereign customer, is the authentication process Sowell alludes to, at least as it relates to product and service offerings. Any offering not valued by customers will be ruthlessly repudiated in a free-market environment, whereas ideas tossed around capriciously by social scientists—such as Karl Marx—have no swift or certain authentication process, especially if they can appeal to enough people's emotional predispositions.

DEVELOPING A THEORY

When Milton Friedman taught his graduate seminar courses in economics at the University of Chicago, he used to ask what his students came to call his two terrifying questions:

How do you know?

So what?

In terms of building a theory, these questions are profound: the first making us observe the world, the second forcing us to say what the effect is. In order to answer the latter, we need theory—a statement of cause and effect. Philosophers of science, such as Karl Popper and Thomas Kuhn, have explained how to build a theory, which is done in a cyclical pattern, as follows:

Observation

Categorization

Prediction

Confirmation

As Nobel Prize-winning economist George Stigler wrote:

In the long run nothing is more essential to a theory than that it be right, but we cannot even pause for a new sentence before remarking that rightness means limited wrongness. The theory must help in explaining to the world that economics is attempting to understand, and a partial explanation is better than none (Stigler, 1982: 157).

Karl Popper echoed Stigler's thought by stating that a theory that cannot be refuted is not scientific. This is why all scientific theories are formulated in a manner exposing them to being disproved. Scientists always ask, "What would it take to admit your theory is wrong?" If you answer nothing, you are arguing an assertion—a matter of faith—not reason. If you cannot be wrong, you cannot be right either. This is why scientists are constantly looking for anomalies. Indeed, many scientific breakthroughs come from such anomalies, such as the properties of helium seeming to defy gravity, mentioned by Steven Landsburg, in Chapter 7. Many papers in science are titled "An Anomalous Case of . . ." It is an iterative process, a never-ending quest of improvement, since only a better theory can replace an inferior theory. This is what the Scottish philosopher David Hume meant when he wrote, "Knowledge is only ignorance postponed."

Theories are not judged based on their complexity, but rather on their usefulness to predict, prescribe, or explain; or as China's former communist leader Deng Xiaoping used to say: "It doesn't matter if a cat is black or white, so long as it catches mice." Some of the best theories are relatively simple, which is fortunate since life is complex enough. Occam's razor applies: *Entia non sunt multiplicanda praeter necessitatem,* Latin for, "No more things should be presumed to exist than are absolutely necessary." A theory is like a map—a mere way to capture the territory—and a life-size map would be useless (as comedian Steven Wright cracks, "How would you fold it?").

Most economic theories are relatively simple; it is the fallacies that get complicated. It is an unnecessary complication to believe that complex effects must have complex causes. The fact that the Earth tilts on its axis is fairly straightforward, but this certainly causes complex reactions in plants, animals, people, ocean currents, and so forth. Being simple often is the outward sign of depth of thought. Ronald Reagan had a simple idea about the Cold War: America wins, the Soviets lose. We should not confuse a *simple* theory with a *simplistic* one.

If you found the four defects leveled against the management industry by the two editors of *The Economist* at the end of the last chapter harsh, this is their major charge against most management books and consultants. There is a paucity—or downright disdain—of theory, and most of the Occam razors they possess could not cut butter.

For example, a lot of consultants will espouse best practices, which is nothing but *mimicking* the actions of successful companies—also known as benchmarking. Harvard Business School Professor Clayton Christensen humorously points out the flaws in this method in *The Innovator's Solution*:

> Consider, for illustration, the history of man's attempts to fly. Early researchers observed strong correlations between being able to fly and having feathers and wings. Possessing these attributes had a high *correlation* with the ability to fly, but when humans attempted to follow the "best practices" of the most successful flyers by strapping feathered wings onto their arms, jumping off cliffs, and flapping hard, they were not successful. . . . It was not until Bernoulli's study of fluid mechanics

helped him articulate the mechanism through which airfoils create lift that human flight began to be *possible* (Christensen and Raynor, 2003: 14).

Similar to *The Economist* editors, Christensen goes on to level this charge against management research:

> Many writers, and many who think of themselves as serious academics, are so eager to prove the worth of their theories that they studiously avoid the discovery of anomalies. . . . We need to do *anomaly-seeking* research, not anomaly-avoiding research.
>
> We have urged doctoral students who are seeking potentially productive research questions for their thesis research to simply ask when a "fad" theory won't work—for example, "When is process reengineering a bad idea?" (ibid: 27).
>
> Unfortunately, many of those engaged in management research seem anxious not to spotlight instances their theory did not accurately predict. They engage in anomaly-avoiding, rather than anomaly-seeking, research and as a result contribute to the perpetuation of unpredictability. Hence, we lay much responsibility for the perceived unpredictability of business building at the feet of the very people whose business it is to study and write about these problems (ibid: 28).

In their endless quest to provide practical, nontheoretical tools executives can use on Monday morning, consultants are doing a disservice to their customers. If we want practical, hands-on learning, let us get a job or go to a trade school; but if we desire insight and wisdom, we should follow the advice of physicist David Bohm and "hang our assumptions in front of us." Henry Mintzberg, Professor of Management Studies at McGill University in Montreal, Canada, explains in his enlightening and provocative book, *Managers Not MBAs,* why theory is an essential part of education:

> Managers who are doing their job live practice every day. They hardly need the educational setting to get them more practical. Education is hands-*off;* otherwise it is not education. It has to provide something different—conceptual ideas that are quite literally *un*realistic and *im*practical, at least seemingly so in conventional terms. People learn when they *suspend their disbeliefs,* to entertain provocative ideas that can reshape their thinking. That is what education is all about.
>
> Certainly managers have to be "practical"—they have to get things done. But they also have to be thoughtful. The best of them think for themselves. . . . The worst copy others—not learn from others, just copy them, mindlessly. They look for some external secret to managerial success, some formula or technique, without realizing that this itself

is a formula for failure. Put differently, a central purpose of management education is to encourage the development of wisdom. This requires a thoughtful atmosphere in the classroom, where individuals can probe into their own experience, primed by interesting ideas, concepts, theories.

Theory is a dirty word in some managerial quarters. That is rather curious, because all of us, managers especially, can no more get along without theories than libraries can get along without catalogs—and for the same reason: theories help us make sense of incoming information.

It would be nice if we could carry reality around in our heads and use it to make our decisions. Unfortunately, no head is that big. So we carry around theories, or models, instead: conceptual frameworks that simplify the reality to help us understand it. Hence, these theories better be good! (Mintzberg, 2004: 249).

Managers these days are inundated with prescriptions. These are the problem in management, not the solution, because situations vary so widely. Who would go to a drugstore that dispenses one kind of pill? So why do managers go to courses that prescribe one kind of technique, the solution for every company, whether strategic planning or share-holder value? What managers need is descriptive insight to help them choose or develop prescriptions for their own particular needs. The fact is that better description in the mind of the intelligent practitioner is the most powerful prescriptive tool we have, for no manager can be better than the conceptual frameworks he or she uses. That is the basis of wisdom (ibid: 252).

Another reason theories are subject to constant falsification is they can show *correlation* but not necessarily *causation,* as Christensen's example of man attempting to fly by attaching feathers and leaping off cliffs proves. In Britain, the number of ham radio operator licenses granted annually was highly correlated with the number of people certified insane, illustrating how a statistically significant result can be insignificant, especially if not illuminated by a theory. Many people die in hospitals, but that does not prove hospitals *cause* death. Wet streets do not cause rain.

One of the most cited anecdotes regarding correlation and causation, and how selection bias in the data we assemble can lead to false conclusions, comes from statistician Abraham Wald, who assessed the vulnerability of airplanes to enemy fire during World War II. The data showed certain parts of the plane were hit more than others, and the military concluded these parts should be reinforced. Wald, however, came to the opposite conclusion, advising to protect the parts hit least often. He understood the *selection bias* inherent in the military's data, which was based on those planes that had returned safely to the air base. Wald figured planes hit in a critical spot would not be likely to return, whereas those that did were hit in noncritical areas. Thus, reinforcing parts on the returned planes would not increase their safety.

Theory and measurement obviously depend on each other, but clearly theory is the senior partner. A correct theory combined with a measurement is impregnable; a measurement without a theory is a statistical orphan.

Let us next discover the difference between pantometry—counting for the sake of counting—and counting when it is coupled with a theory to see how the superiority of the scientific method can be applied to the corporation.

9

PANTOMETRY VERSUS THEORY

Mathematics has no symbols for confused ideas.

—George Stigler, Nobel Laureate economist

To know the future, we would have to know today what we will know tomorrow. Not a very likely scenario for most of us who do not believe in prognosticators or false prophets. The only viable method for peering into the future is with a theory, and since in a business context we are dealing with humans—mercurial creatures whose actions are beyond the reach of mere calculations—the most we can hope for is to constantly test and refine our theories in order to gain a better understanding of human behavior.

At the macroeconomic level, business-cycle theory has been a preoccupation of economists ever since economic activity has been recorded. Understanding where the economy has been, where it is, and where it is heading has confounded economists and politicians for centuries. To help them wrestle with this issue, economists have been refining their theories and using economic indicators to help enrich their understanding of macroeconomic cycles.

BUSINESS-CYCLE THEORY

Why did God create economists?
Answer: To make weather forecasters look good.

—Old economist's joke

As the Scientific Management Revolution championed by Frederick Taylor expanded from businesses to governments, the economics profession around the world was developing national income and production statistics accounting to measure macroeconomic activity. In the United States, Simon Kuznets

(1901–1985), a Russian-born economist and Harvard professor, invented the gross national product (now commonly known as the gross domestic product) in the early 1940s. In 1971, he won the Nobel Prize for his seminal statistical work on national income.

Once we began to measure the economic performance of a national economy, the next logical step was to begin to *forecast* the performance of the economy. To be able to do this, economists had to develop a plethora of economic indicators to measure where the economy was heading, by looking at where it had been. There is no reason to discuss how these indicators came about, or even their validity. Instead, we will focus on the various indicators and the different purposes they serve.

Some economic indicators provide a snapshot of the economy's health. Similar to the way a doctor checks your vital signs, an economist might check the vital signs of the economy by looking at changes in gross domestic product (GDP), consumer price index (CPI), national income, or the unemployment rate. Unlike management accountants and auditors, who tend to focus on lagging indicators—such as a business's financial statements—economists developed not only *lagging indicators,* but also *leading* and *coincident indicators.*

- *Leading indicators* anticipate the direction in which the economy is headed.
- *Coincident indicators* provide information about the current status of the economy.
- *Lagging indicators* change months after a downturn or upturn in the economy.

The terms *leading, coincident,* and *lagging* refer to the timing of the turning points of the indexes relative to those of the business cycle. These indicators change as the economy moves from one phase of the business cycle to the next and tell economists that an upturn or downturn in the economy has arrived. Lagging indicators change months after a downturn or upturn in the economy has begun and help economists predict the duration of swings in the cycle.

Here are the definitions of the three different types of indicators (originally produced by the Department of Commerce), now tracked by the privately run Conference Board, from its Web site:

> The composite indexes of leading, coincident, and lagging indicators produced by The Conference Board are summary statistics for the U.S. economy. They are constructed by averaging their individual components in order to smooth out a good part of the volatility of the individual

series. Historically, the cyclical turning points in the leading index have occurred before those in aggregate economic activity, cyclical turning points in the coincident index have occurred at about the same time as those in aggregate economic activity, and cyclical turning points in the lagging index generally have occurred after those in aggregate economic activity.

Leading Indicators: Anticipate a Business Cycle

Average weekly hours, manufacturing

Average weekly initial claims for unemployment insurance

Manufacturers' new orders, consumer goods and materials

Vendor performance, slower deliveries diffusion index

Manufacturers' new orders, nondefense capital goods

Building permits, new private housing units

Stock prices, 500 common stocks

Money supply, M2

Interest rate spread, 10-year Treasury bonds less federal funds

Index of consumer expectations

Coincident Indicators: Run in Sync with Business Cycle

Employees on nonagricultural payrolls

Personal income less transfer payments

Industrial production

Manufacturing and trade sales

Lagging Indicators: Follow Changes in Business Cycle

Average duration of unemployment

Inventories to sales ratio, manufacturing and trade

Labor cost per unit of output, manufacturing

Average prime rate

Commercial and industrial loans

Consumer installment credit to personal income ratio

Consumer price index for services

(*Source:* Conference Board Web site: www.conference-board.org/economics/bci/component.cfm, accessed February 2, 2006.)

This is not to claim economists can predict the future; far from it. There is a tremendous amount of history that supports the observation that no one can predict the future. For an insightful book on this subject, see *The Experts Speak,* by Christopher Cerf and Victor Navasky, of the Institute of Expertology, whose sole purpose is to collect predictions from prominent people and publish them for posterity. That said, the indicators just described no doubt have expanded our knowledge of how an economy operates, and may even provide a clue as to where it is heading, but they are still a compendium of averages, and averages can be very misleading—you can drown in a lake that is, on average, four feet deep. Further, the debate over which indicators should be used is by no means settled theory. Keynesian economists focus on demand-side indicators; monetarists focus on the money supply; and supply-siders concentrate on business investment, entrepreneurial growth, marginal tax rates, venture capital investments, and production. Henry Hazlitt (1894–1993), who wrote the classic *Economics in One Lesson,* expressed the objective of studying economics as well as anyone: "The main purpose of economics is not to predict the future, but to learn what policies are likely to improve that future."

YOUR FICO SCORE IS A THEORY

Fair Isaac transformed the credit industry by pioneering the use of credit scoring in the late 1950s, known as *predictive analytics* (also, *prescriptive analytics*). Credit providers who used to manually review each application could now rely on credit scores, providing a scalable alternative and ushering in a wave of growth in many industries, while granting customers increased access to credit. According to the Fair Isaac Web site: "Throughout the 1960s and into the 1970s, Fair Isaac popularized credit scoring one company at a time. It took more than a decade of cold calls on skeptical lenders before banks began to see the possibilities. But by the early 1980s, credit scoring had become an industry standard in the United States, and was also used by forward-thinking institutions in many other countries" (www.fairisaac.com/Fairisaac/Solutions/innovations_predictive_modeling7.htm, accessed February 5, 2006).

Your individual FICO—Fair Isaac Corporation—score is comprised of five weighted components that have been tested to have predictive capabilities about your future creditworthiness:

Payment history (35 percent)

Amounts owed (30 percent)

Length of credit history (15 percent)

New credit (10 percent)

Types of credit used (10 percent)

Notice the FICO score is not simply a measurement. It certainly contains measurements, but it is driven by a theory of which characteristics can predict future behavior. This is the essential difference between measuring for the sake of measuring and a measure that is enlightened by a theory.

Recall that a theory should be able to explain, predict, or prescribe certain outcomes or behaviors. The Conference Board and FICO indicators noted previously attempt to do just that—they are theories, testable in the real world to see how well they accomplish those three goals. If the theories are falsified, they are then revised and tested again. Frederick Taylor developed theories for improving productivity, which were tested in factories the world over and found to be valid. It is a much easier task to develop a set of indicators for a particular business, or an individual's creditworthiness, than it is for an entire economy, as the anomalies in per capita GDP illustrate.

DOES PER CAPITA GDP MEASURE HAPPINESS AND WELL-BEING?

Focusing on measurements, without theory, can lead to ridiculous, and sometimes deadly, conclusions. This is why the McKinsey maxim—what you can

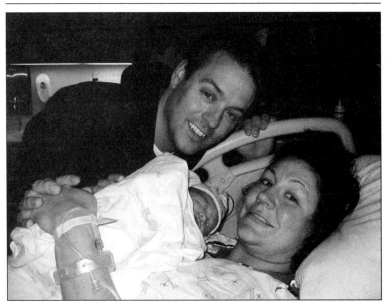

Exhibit 9.1   Why are Christine and Ed so happy? Their per capita household income just decreased by one-third with the birth of Sean Michael.

Photo by Donna Heidenreich

measure you can manage—is such sophistry. For the ridiculous, consider the GDP, the output produced *within* a country's borders. GDP counts spending on a child's education as consumption, even though this investment in human capital is acknowledged to pay dividends for decades to come. If there is a construction boom in New Orleans due to the devastation caused by Hurricane Katrina, or due to an increase in desire to live in the Big Easy, the GDP counts them equally.

National income accounting ignores many personal factors of well-being and standard of living, such as leisure time and environmental quality. Divorce, for instance, causes GDP to increase, since two cars, two homes, two sets of toys, and so on, are now required in place of one. Some measures of success hide other types of failure. In fairness, though, the GDP was never meant to be the definitive measure of economic welfare.

If we take a country's GDP and divide it by the population, we get per capita GDP, a measurement of the wealth of a country. But this measurement alone can lead to preposterous conclusions. When a sheep is born, GDP goes up, supposedly increasing our per capita wealth. But when a child is born, our per capita GDP *goes down*.

DEADLY MEASURES

For an example of more serious consequences deriving from an obsession with numerical measurements, consider Robert McNamara, America's Secretary of Defense during the Vietnam War. In his own words, he possessed "a limited grasp of military affairs, and even less grasp of covert operations." He brought the same mental model to this job that he used at the Ford Motor Company, where he was one of the so-called Whiz Kids hired by Ford to deal with its sagging profits.

Because to McNamara the numbers told the entire story of the war, his systems analysis, the Planning-Programming-Budgeting System (PPBS), was heavy on measurement and rational analysis. According to an article in the *New York Times Magazine,* "During the war [McNamara] was so impressed by the logic of statistics that he tried to calculate how many deaths it would take to bring North Vietnam to the bargaining table" (Shipler, 1997).

McNamara could count the casualties and kill ratios, but could not deal with the more difficult, uncertain, and subjective issues of war—matters that required insight and wisdom, not just statistics. The numbers gave him a false sense of security, since the kill ratios showed the U.S. military was winning battles and inflicting *numerically* more deaths on the enemy than it was suffering. McNamara could count the bodies but couldn't describe what was happening in the war, much like the difference between poring over marketing reports rather than getting out and talking to customers.

McNamara finally admitted in his mea culpa that hard analysis often leads to overweighting the knowledge you have. Things that can't be measured, such human factors as judgment, ethics, and intuition, usually make the most important difference between good and bad decisions.

We have a similar situation when we rely too heavily on accounting reports to assess the health of our businesses. As Enron, WorldCom, and other accounting scandals teach, a company's financial statements can be manipulated to present a good picture, all the while covering up the reality behind the numbers and forestalling corrective actions taken by the marketplace, like bankruptcy.

ACCOUNTING IS NOT A THEORY

Today's pantometrists—accountants—focus their attention on the three traditional financial statements: the balance sheet, income statement, and statement of cash flows. These are all examples of *lagging* indicators, as they report on where a particular business has been. This may or may not be useful in determining where the business is heading. If users extrapolate financial reports into the future, they are relying on an implicit theory: the past will equal the future. A dubious notion.

Real-time financial statements would rise to the level of *coincident* indicators, since they would track present performance. But what every business should develop is a set of *leading* indicators that would enable them to get a sense of which direction the business is heading. The accounting profession proffers little help in achieving this objective, for a very fundamental reason: accounting is not a theory.

Developing leading indicators requires evolving a set of falsifiable theories the business can test to determine the relationship between those indicators and future financial performance. The accounting profession has simply not taken the lead in this area. The reason may be explained by a joke told by a graduate economics student:

> One day in microeconomics, the professor was writing up the typical "underlying assumptions" in preparation to explain a new model. I turned to my friend and asked, "What would economics be without assumptions?" He thought for a moment, then replied, "Accounting."

When Fra Luca Pacioli introduced double-entry bookkeeping in 1494, it was no doubt a revolutionary concept, as it allowed businesses to expand beyond familial and geographical boundaries. Accounting to this day states, quite rightly, that debits must always equal credits. That is, it is an identity statement, expressed in the following fundamental accounting equation taught in every beginning bookkeeping course:

$$\text{Assets} - \text{Liabilities} = \text{Owner's Equity}$$

An identity statement is true due to its definition. It is not a theory. A demand curve is an example of an identity statement: the summation of how much product customers would purchase at various prices. The supply curve is the same: a summation of how much product businesses would be willing to provide at various prices. It was not until economists combined these two identities into the scissors of the well-known supply and demand graph—inserting some assumptions along the way—that they posited the *theory of supply and demand.*

The principles of accounting also do not comprise a theory; rather they are simply a set of guidelines, rules, and procedures for measuring financial items such as assets, liabilities, revenues, and expenses, grounded by standards such as relevance, reliability, and materiality.

One cannot use the accounting equation to predict the future of a business anymore than one can use the federal government's budget deficit, or trade deficit, as a predictive tool. It is not the equation or the measurement that provides the usefulness; it is the context of the assumptions behind it that matter. Milton Friedman used to point out that he would rather live in a world where the government spent $1 trillion and ran a $500 million budget deficit than one where the government spent $2 trillion with a balanced budget, since the true cost of government is what it spends, not its budget deficit. Whether you agree with him or not is a value judgment, based on how you view the usefulness of government spending. The numbers, in and of themselves, do not provide enough context to draw any insightful conclusions.

Is it any wonder the accounting profession has not taken the lead in movements such as the Balanced Scorecard, which attempts to look at more indicators than merely historical financial performance metrics? Yet every executive team should develop a set of leading indicators—canaries in the coal mine—they can use to properly lead the business to profitability and excellence, our next topic.

10

MEASURES THAT MATTER

Answers aren't just found in numbers.
You have to get out and look.

—A.G. Lafley, CEO, Procter & Gamble

Modern-day businesses are built on an edifice of numbers. The rationalists with MBAs and CPAs continue to widen their numerical abstractions of how a business should be managed, imposing this worldview on executives until management has transmogrified into an autistic science, dominated by numbers, rather than adding value and serving the needs of flesh-and-blood human beings.

We have all heard the clichés: What you can measure you can manage. If you can't measure it, it's not worth doing. People do what you *inspect,* not what you *expect.* We are what we measure. People do what you count, not necessarily what counts. Ad nauseam. Yet this metric mania misses many oblique things in the real world, because it crowds out insight, intuition, judgment, creativity, and imagination. These characteristics are sometimes the most feared among executives since they seem to imply chaos, imbalance, lack of discipline, and other disorderly behavior.

But it is precisely these emotional traits that are the primary sources of creativity. Most great scientists agree they never discovered anything with their rational mind alone, citing intuition as being more important than intelligence. Einstein's famous saying, "Imagination is more important than knowledge," elaborates this point.

Indeed, Einstein was famous for his *Gedanken*—thought experiments—and credits using his imagination to envision himself traveling on a light beam, which led to his discovery of relativity. In today's frenetic corporations, demanding more and more output with fewer and fewer inputs, this type of creativity is too little rewarded. It certainly doesn't improve the Taylorite productivity statistics executives are so enamored with. Average workers are so busy *doing* they do not have the time to *reflect* on what they have done, let alone discover major breakthroughs. But action without reflection is meaningless, as the T.S. Eliot poem expresses well: "We had the experience but missed the meaning." In Latin, "reflect" comes from the verb meaning *refold,* implying the action of turning things inward in order to see them in a different way.

This is precisely the type of reflection needed for any company to develop its own key predictive indicators. Note that I am drawing a distinction between a key *performance* indicator and a key *predictive* indicator. A performance indicator is a measurement, such as the number of customer complaints or patents filed, but lacks a falsifiable theory. A predictive indicator, by contrast, is a measurement supported by a theory, which can be tested and refined, in order to explain, prescribe, or predict behavior. As discussed previously, we are interested in developing theories, and measuring factors that are dictated by that theory, rather than measuring for the sake of measuring. Utilizing Einstein's method of a thought experiment is a good place to start.

A GEDANKEN

Engage in this thought experiment. You are the CEO of Continental Airlines: Which leading indicators would you want to look at on a daily—or even hourly or shorter—basis to determine whether or not Continental was fulfilling its mission of flying passengers around the world profitably? It is relatively easy to develop *lagging* indicators, such as profit, revenue per passenger mile, cost per passenger mile, repeat customer bookings, frequent flyer miles earned, and so on. But because they are lagging indicators, all of the employees would not be able to influence those results on a day-to-day basis. How would the baggage handler's behavior change as a result of learning last month's load factor? We need some canaries in the airline to serve as leading indicators of performance.

You could certainly develop *coincident* indicators, by tracking in real time all of the lagging indicators mentioned; and no doubt the airlines do this internally to some extent. But that still does not necessarily help the pilots, flight crews, baggage handlers, or food service caterers fulfill the goals and objectives of the airline on an hour-by-hour timeline. What are needed are leading indicators—theories—that have some *predictive* power; in other words, they predict the financial results of Continental.

In his book, *From Worst to First: Behind the Scenes of Continental's Remarkable Comeback,* Gordon Bethune details how he was able to turn around the failed airline (which had filed for Chapter 7 bankruptcy twice in the preceding decade) between February 1994 and 1997, turning it into one of the best and most profitable airlines in the sky. It is a remarkable story, and it illustrates the importance of utilizing leading key predictive indicators (KPIs) to focus the entire organization on its purpose and mission. Bethune tracked, daily, three leading KPIs:

- On-time arrival
- Lost luggage
- Customer complaints

When Bethune became CEO, Continental ranked dead last in all of these indicators, which are also measured by the Department of Transportation (known as the "Triple Crown Criteria"). Bethune analyzed the problems—and there were many—and discovered the culture of the airline was focused on driving down cost per available seat mile (the standard measure of cost in the airline industry). It cut costs at every opportunity, by packing the planes with more seats, reducing the food and drink portions, paying its people poorly, and so forth. It believed its mission was to cut costs; but as Bethune constantly pointed out, "We aren't in business to save money, we are in business to put out a good product. . . . You can make a pizza so cheap nobody wants to eat it. And you can make an airline so cheap nobody wants to fly it" (Bethune, 1998: 123, 50). There is an enormous difference between controlling costs and being cheap. A business must make investments that deliver value to the customer.

This harkens back to Peter Drucker's concept of the purpose of a business: to innovate and create wealth for its customers, not simply to be efficient. What makes the three indicators just listed leading is that they measure success the same way the customer does. And that is critical because, ultimately, the success of any business is a result of loyal customers who return. In other words, profit is a lagging indicator of what is in the hearts and minds of your customers. A leading indicator, at its most valuable, measures success the same way the customer does. None of the three indicators would show up on a financial statement, but, as the airlines have learned over the years—by testing the theory—they have a predictive correlation with profits. Any indicator that can be gleaned from a financial statement is most likely a lagging—or at best, coincident—indicator, since leading indicators are nonfinancial in nature. The other important point about the three indicators is that *every* employee of Continental can influence the outcome of each of them, from the baggage handlers and flight crews to the gate agents and reservation operators. It is worth quoting Bethune at length on this vital point:

Before I came to work at Continental, the company wanted to be a successful airline. But it measured only one thing: cost. That made Continental an airline that ran on low cost, paid its employees poorly, and delivered a really, really crappy product. That was not what our customers wanted (ibid: 233).

Don't forget, Continental got what it seemed to want at the time: By saying that cost was the thing that defined its success, Continental's management got everybody to focus on cost. That turned out to be the wrong thing to focus on, though, and they just couldn't get that through their heads. It was what they focused on, it was what they measured, and they simply believed that somehow it would lead to success. That's why, even before the organization almost gave up the ghost, even when it was still trying as hard as it could, Continental just couldn't find the key to success—because the key didn't reside in cost, and cost was the main thing Continental focused on (ibid: 233).

When we're looking for goals for an entire company, we make sure our employees know what we're going for: to get the planes on time, not to aim for a certain return on investment. Goals such as certain equity or debt ratios or interest percentages work fine for the accountants, just as striving to repair a specific number of engines or reduce the number of seconds before the phone gets answered are goals set for particular departments. But when it concerns the whole company, we need a companywide goal—something that employees can immediately identify (ibid: 208).

At the risk of oversimplifying, this is basically the key to running a successful business. You have to decide what constitutes success. If it's a fishing contest, are we trying to catch the heaviest fish or the longest fish? If it's a baseball game, what makes an out and what scores a run? If it's an airline, what are the indications that it is doing well? You have to explain to the people who work with you what those are, and the people have to buy into that. You have to measure that, and let them know how you're going to measure it. And you have to reward them if they succeed. That's it (ibid: 232).

Your employees are very smart. They pay close attention. What you're measuring and rewarding, they're going to do. So even if you define success right but you still measure and reward the wrong thing, your employees are going to figure out what you're measuring and give you that. If we had said that our goal was to be a great airline that gets its planes to their destinations on time and treats its customers right, but we also said that we were going to measure that by checking attendance very closely and making sure that people followed the rules of the employee manual [which Bethune burned in the parking lot upon becoming CEO] to the letter, we would have had the best goal in the world, but we would have ended up with very prompt employees who kept their noses in their manuals. And, probably, we would have had a pretty lousy airline (ibid: 234).

This is one of the most common problems in businesses. Businesses fail because they want the right things but measure the wrong things— or they measure the right things in the wrong way, so they get the wrong results. Remember? Define success the way your customers define it (ibid: 233).

Obviously, the KPIs for the airline industry will evolve over time, since they deal with customer expectations, which are dynamic, not static. And because these KPIs are an actual theory, they must constantly be tested and falsified, and new ones developed to reflect changing market conditions. These KPIs are not only critical for internal management, but also are important as information that outside investors and other third parties are interested in to assess the health and direction of the business. Employee and customer loyalty information, sales and marketing success measurements, brand value, percentage of revenue derived from new products offered, number of patents received, and a host of other measurements that one cannot find on the company's financial statements are beginning to be demanded by third parties. If you think KPIs are relevant only to businesses, read the sidebar, "Baseball KPIs." Notice how the "conventional wisdom" within baseball rejects these new theories, yet they have predictive ability. (For more on baseball KPIs, see the review of *Moneyball*, by Michael Lewis, in Suggested Reading at the end of this book).

Baseball KPIs
by Ed Kless, Senior Fellow, VeraSage Institute

In baseball, conventional wisdom believes that a player whose batting average is over .300 is successful; a season total of more that 80 runs batted in, a good one; at 15 home runs season, a decent power hitter. Problems occur when we try to extrapolate the success of the player's team based on these individual accomplishments or try to predict the future success of the player based on these statistics.

Wins do not come from individual accomplishment, but rather the performance of the team—specifically, the team's ability to produce runs on offense and limit runs on defense. In fact, a causal relationship exists between the number of runs scored and allowed by a team and the team's winning percentage. This is one of the "Known Principles of Sabermetrics"

(continues)

as defined by Bill James in the *1984 Baseball Abstract*. James, an economist by trade, developed the Pythagorean win-loss percentage calculation, so called because of its similarity to the Pythagorean theorem in
geometry, $a^2 + b^2 = c^2$.

Calculated by squaring the team's runs scored then dividing by the
square of runs scored plus the square of the team's runs allowed, the
Pythagorean win-loss percentage is an estimate of a team's winning percentage given its runs scored and runs allowed.

$$Predicted\ winning\ percentage = Runs\ Scored^2$$
$$\div\ (Runs\ Scored^2 + Runs)\ Allowed^2$$

This understanding dispels the myths of fans everywhere that their
team is only a few lucky breaks away from seriously improving their
performance. A common gris-gris is that a team could have completely
changed its performance in a season by just winning a few more of
the one-run games with a lucky break here or there. Nothing could be
further from the truth.

What this does mean is crucial. Wins are a function of runs scored
less runs allowed. A baseball player's purpose then is to assist in the
creation of runs for his team and/or reduce the runs allowed by his team.
While this seems obvious, it is not to most people involved in baseball
management. Let us look at one of the other great myths perpetuated by
the baseball establishment—the importance of batting average.

To calculate a hitter's batting average, you take the number of hits a
player has made and divide by the total number of at-bats. A .300 hitter
will have stroked a hit 3 times while making an out 7 times (3/10). The main
problem is that batting average does not take into account a player's ability to: (a) get on base without the benefit of a hit (mostly walks) and (b) get
beyond first base.

The first problem is solved by looking at on-base percentage (OBP),
as opposed to batting average. On-base percentage differs from batting
average in that OBP measures a player's ability to get on base regardless
of how. In other words, it includes walks and the number of times the
player was hit by a pitch. While these are less glamorous than hits, they
are nonetheless important for two reasons: (1) It is a more accurate rep-
resentation of the player's ability to help create runs; and (2) when inverted,
OBP demonstrates the player's ability not to make an out, thereby keeping an inning going and increasing the chances for the team to score runs.

The second problem, getting beyond first base, is solved by looking
at slugging percentage rather than batting average. Slugging percentage

measures the total bases achieved by the player from the original hit. To calculate slugging percentage, one needs to first calculate total bases. A player receives one base for a single, two for a double, three for a triple, and four for a home run. One then adds these together and divides by at-bats.

In the late 1970s, Bill James put these two statistics together to develop a new statistic, on-base plus slugging. He further extrapolated from these two measures a concept called *runs created*. We will not clutter these pages with how the calculations are made; however, it needs to be expressed that once one can calculate approximately how many runs a player creates, one can then answer some interesting questions. One such question is, How would a team comprised of clones of one player perform against a team of clones of another player?

Taking an example from a recent baseball season, we will compare the statistics of two outfielders: Brian Giles of the Arizona Diamondbacks and Carl Crawford of the Tampa Bay Devil Rays. According to traditional baseball wisdom, these players could not be more similar.

Player	GP	BA	HR	RBI
Brian Giles	158	.301	15	83
Carl Crawford	156	.301	15	81

Both batted .301 with 15 home runs and just over 80 runs batted in while playing in almost the same number of games. Many traditionalists would look at these players and believe they would have almost the same value to their respective teams. However, looking more closely at on-base percentage and slugging percentage, we would find the following:

Player	OBP	SLG	RC/27 Outs
Brian Giles	.423	.483	7.41
Carl Crawford	.331	.469	5.57

While the difference between the players' slugging percentage is a small factor, the key difference is on-base percentage. The two are separated by .092, mostly on the strength of Giles's 119 walks (not exactly a glamour statistic). More importantly, when we calculate the number of runs created by each player using James's formula, we see that Giles creates almost two more runs per 27 outs. Twenty-seven outs is one offensive game (three outs per inning times nine innings per game). Remember, the effect of a walk is compounded because in addition to reaching base, a walk is not an out, thereby prolonging the inning.

Since we also know from league statistics what the average number of runs per game for the leagues are, we now can compute how a team composed of all Gileses and all Crawfords would perform against the rest of the league. Giles played in the National League where the average number of runs scored per team per game is 4.45. Crawford played in the American League where, because a designated hitter bats in place of a usually weak-hitting pitcher, the average number of runs per team per game is a higher 4.76.

By running these numbers through the Pythagorean win-loss percentage calculation, we would compute the following:

Player	W	L	%	GB
Team of Brian Gileses	119	43	.735	—
Team of Carl Crawfords	94	68	.578	25

No doubt, a team of Carl Crawfords would perform quite well; but in a league with a team of Brian Gileses, they would finish 25 games behind. Clearly looking at the correct key performance indicator makes a huge difference in baseball. The same is true in business.

DEFINING SUCCESS THE SAME WAY CUSTOMERS DO

The most important function of the KPIs is to define success the same way the customer does. The problem with so many accounting and management systems is they are built upon a supreme rationality of *internal* business metrics, but are not focused on the external value received, as defined by the customer. This is not to say these two objectives are mutually exclusive, as there is no doubt that some internal objectives will intersect with external customer definitions of success. For instance, lost luggage is estimated to cost the airline industry approximately $1 billion per year, plus incalculable loss of goodwill; improving that KPI not only pleases customers, it also reduces internal waste, a worthy goal. The difference, though, between a KPI and other lagging indicators is that the former should be the talisman that guides organizational action, to align internal activity with external value created. This positing, testing, falsifying, and refining of KPIs is no easy task; it requires an incredible amount of thought and creativity and necessitates challenging an organization's basic assumptions of how it performs and delivers its value proposition. It cannot be done by focusing on measurements alone; you have to understand what is valuable to customers.

NO RIGHT WAY TO DO THE WRONG THING

During the 1980s, Total Quality Management (TQM) swept the business literature, and many companies rushed to institute a TQM program. TQM is a body of knowledge that dates back to the late 1800s, as part of the agricultural revolution. Yet applying TQM to a knowledge business is no easy task, since it is a standards-based approach. Karl Albrecht has always been a strong critic of TQM, especially as it applies to a service business, as he pointed out in *The Northbound Train: Finding the Purpose, Setting the Direction, Shaping the Destiny of Your Organization*:

> Too many quality efforts begin as administrative, analytical, mechanistic, control-oriented, dehumanized, standards-based management attempts to "tighten up" the organization rather than loosen it up and empower the people to make their own individual quality commitments. This is why the doctrinaire, mechanistic TQM systems are ultimately doomed to failure (Albrecht, 1994: 32–33).

Albrecht then offers an example of an insurance company that invested heavily in a performance standard it considered important: a five-day turnaround in issuing policies, 90 percent of the time (ibid: 139). This is the perfect project for a TQM model because it can be counted, measured against a standard, analyzed, constantly improved, and so forth. The only problem was, when Albrecht's consulting firm talked with the insurance agents and their customers, nobody cared about receiving their policies within five days.

What is the point? There is really no right way to do the wrong thing. As Peter Drucker wrote: "Nothing is so useless as doing efficiently that which should not be done at all," which is why we have replaced efficiency with effectiveness in the new business equation, discussed in Chapter 4. From a customer value proposition perspective, the breakdown here is easy to diagnose: TQM is an inside-out approach. The organization can internally count, measure, and analyze against almost any standard. But weighing yourself 10 times a day will not reduce your weight. TQM may provide a scale but not the guiding light for what should be weighed. Some companies have embraced TQM largely because it utilizes mathematical and statistical methods we easily understand. But we need to shift our thinking from "everything begins and ends with management" to "everything begins and ends with customer value." Counting and measuring things for the sake of counting and measuring things will not be the *open sesame* to attracting and retaining customers.

The alternative to TQM is Total Quality Service (TQS), which Albrecht defined as: "A state of affairs in which an organization delivers superior value to its stakeholders: its customers, its owners, and its employees" (Albrecht, 1992: 72). Notice how this definition is a goal condition to be sought, not a particular method of operation. Methods are developed as a way to achieve the goal, not as ends in themselves. The reason TQS is a better beacon than TQM for intellectual capital companies is that it recognizes the subjective value of what is delivered, not the objective quality. Customers expect their products to work; TQS puts the focus and emphasis on the subjective value and the service experience, the ultimate arbiters of whether the customer remains a customer. As Stanley Marcus used to admonish: "Service, or the lack of it, doesn't come through on the computer printouts; it has to be observed" (Marcus, 1979: 42).

There is a sign in the textile plant of the Baldrige National Quality Award-winning Milliken & Company that reads, "Quality is not the absence of defects as defined by management, but the presence of value as defined by customers." Motorola, Inc., another Baldrige winner, has gained a world-wide reputation striving for Six Sigma quality (as did General Electric, especially under the tenure of Jack Welch). It is an impressive standard, and Motorola has been able to achieve this in many aspects of its operations. But what happens when they achieve that impressive goal? Does that automatically give them customer loyalty or guarantee profitability? Zero defects is not enough. In the long run, customers will begin to expect this result and competitors will be able to match this standard. New canaries (theories) will be needed to predict customer behavior. What counts even more than Six Sigma quality is how Motorola treats its customers, for as Donald E. Peterson, former chairman of Ford Motor Co., said upon bringing that company back from the precipice of poor financial performance: "If we aren't customer-driven, our cars won't be either." Given Ford's current financial problems, it seems this proclamation has been forgotten.

To make this undertaking of developing KPIs even more challenging, no two businesses will use the exact same indicators, although certain standards may be established for an industry, such as the "Triple Crown Criteria" discussed for the airlines. Dell computer, for instance, has developed a customer dashboard that measures three critical success factors for its business: order fulfillment, product performance, and service support. These critical success factors are sometimes referred to as a dashboard because they serve the same purpose the dashboard in an automobile does: they inform the driver of the key indicators that you want to constantly monitor and are essential to keep the car moving forward—fuel capacity, RPMs, temperature, oil pressure, and so forth. Automotive canaries, to use our analogy.

Lexus considers the lifetime ownership costs an essential KPI for the customer, and it works diligently to drive down the lifetime costs of owning a Lexus. This is accomplished by using high-quality parts in the design, and the development of the Certified Pre-Owned Auto Program so dealers can recondition used cars and offer a manufacturer's warranty for up to 100,000 miles, thereby increasing the resale value of a Lexus, which lowers the lifetime cost of ownership. Lexus's parent company, Toyota, also uses this lifetime ownership cost as a KPI.

Another example of a company that has defined success the same way as the customer is one that most likely every reader of this book has patronized at least once.

IT'S 12:41 A.M.: DO YOU KNOW WHERE YOUR PACKAGE—AND CPA—ARE?

It is September 9, 2002, and two CPAs depart at noon from two different Bay Area airports; they converge on Memphis, Tennessee International Airport by 10:00 P.M. that evening. Precisely at 10:30 P.M. they are met by Karl, the manager of Quality & Process Improvement, at FedEx. As they drive around the Memphis terminal and approach the 400-acre FedEx facility, they are taken aback by its enormous size. They enter the facility at 11:15 P.M., are met and greeted warmly by various FedEx representatives, given guest name badges, and ushered through metal detectors—this is, after all, an airport—and into the central hub of FedEx.

That night, approximately 174 aircraft from points around the world will land in Memphis, as 9,000 FedEx team members unload, sort, and reload between 1.2 and 1.5 million packages. All of this activity will take place between 10:30 P.M. and 4:45 A.M. in an amazing display of coordination, efficiency, timeliness, and effectiveness. More than 400 miles of conveyors will be used to sort the packages as they pass through laser scanners that capture a wealth of information, such as the destination address that guides each package from the primary sort to the secondary sort area. There are video terminals everywhere showing the countdown and projected times various flights must be loaded in order to make the demanding on-time delivery goals (talk about customer canaries). The CPAs are shown the central control room where all of the estimated times are counted and tracked, and all the problems are handled.

At some point past 4:00 A.M. the planes are loaded and the pilots await word from the control center. In 90-second bursts, each plane takes off for its respective destination, its packages to be unloaded and placed onto a fleet of more than 50,000 delivery vehicles throughout the world and hand-carried to their destinations. Approximately one-half of the total volume of FedEx passes through the Memphis hub, with the remaining 50 percent processed in mini-hubs throughout the country.

It is the FedEx value statement of People–Service–Profits put in motion every night. The tour guide explains the only assumption not challenged is how FedEx treats its people; everything else is open to experimentation and falsification to improve the customer experience. As the CPAs are shuttled around to the various tour points, they drive past the airplanes and one of them notices a first name painted underneath the pilot's window of each aircraft. He asks if that is the pilot's name and is told, no, it is the name chosen from a lottery drawing in which all FedEx team members are eligible to participate. Each time a plane is painted, a new name is drawn and the plane is dedicated to that person—usually a child of a FedEx team member. The CPAs wonder how it must feel for a ten-year-old to have his or her name on a FedEx airplane!

Most of the 9,000 team members are part-time, and have jobs elsewhere. However, FedEx provides them with full-time equivalent benefits—such as health insurance, 401(k) plan, and a defined benefit pension plan (for example, the CPAs' tour guide works during the day for a not-for-profit and said FedEx was his "retirement"). Printed on every FedEx paycheck envelope is: "A Satisfied Customer Made This Possible."

It is truly an amazing sight, and FedEx has come a long way from its first day of operations on March 12, 1973, when it had only six packages to deliver—four of which were from sales people testing the system, and only two from paying customers. Not bad for Fred Smith, a guy who got a "C" on his term paper that contained the idea for FedEx.

For many years, FedEx operated under the 95 percent rule, which was a curve that showed to improve on-time delivery beyond 95 percent would be cost-prohibitive and would require a price not acceptable to the majority of its customers. Conversely, to drop below 95 percent on-time delivery would also be unacceptable to the customer, so 95 percent was thought to be the optimal operating level, both in profitability and customer service. As Michael Basch explains in his book *Customer Culture: How FedEx and Other Great Companies Put the Customer First Every Day*:

> Fred Smith has a way of standing back from the business and challenging the basic tenets of the business. One day he challenged the "95 percent rule"—a sacred cow since the very early days.

"If we handle a million packages a day and we mess up 5 percent, that means we mess up 50,000 packages a day," he reasoned. "And since one person ships to another, that means we've disappointed 100,000 people each day. It doesn't take a rocket scientist to figure out that before long you've disappointed everyone in America who ships or receives packages."

Then he created what he called a Hierarchy of Horrors. Of the 5 percent disappointments, what is the worst thing you can do to the customer? What is the next worst thing and so on? He and his senior management team identified eight major horrors (Basch, 2002: 162).

By hanging their assumptions in front of them, challenging them, the FedEx team developed the resulting "Hierarchy of Horrors," which was the genesis for the FedEx Service Quality Index (SQI), a series of weighted KPIs that define success the same way the customer does. The SQI measures the following functions, each weighted according to the degree of customer aggravation caused by a failure to perform. The number of "average daily failure points" is multiplied by that component's assigned weight to calculate the SQI:

Item	Weight
Right day late service failures	1
Wrong day late service failures	5
Traces (incomplete package scan data in the computer system)	1
Complaints reopened by customers	5
Missing proof of delivery	1
Invoice adjustments requested	1
Missed pickups	10
Damaged packages	10
Lost packages	10
Overgoods (lost and found)	5
Abandoned calls	1
International SQI	1

(Albrecht and Zemke, 2002: 94)

Since being placed in service in 1987, the SQI has enabled FedEx to increase its on-time delivery performance from 95 percent to 99.7 percent without adding significant marginal costs. FedEx credits team member commitment for achieving this outstanding result, similar to Bethune's turnaround of Continental Airlines by focusing on the Triple Crown criteria.

The most critical technology that enables FedEx, and its customers, to track every single package anywhere in the system is its sophisticated package-tracking system, now known as COSMOS,® for the FedEx Customer-Oriented Service and Management Operating System. COSMOS monitors the movement of all shipments within the FedEx network—more than 3 million each business day. Customers can tap into COSMOS via the Internet to verify a shipment's status—and they do so millions of times each month.

When Fred Smith implemented the tracking system, many asked why he would invest such large sums of money in a technology that would not speed up delivery by one second. In other words, in a Taylorite view of the world of efficiency, there would be no increase in outputs relative to inputs. But that was not the point. By providing FedEx customers real-time access to their package information, he was creating an *excuseless culture* inside FedEx, by designing a system that held all team members accountable to the success factors important to the customer.

As Fred Smith said to the audience at the J.D. Power and Associates Customer Service Conference in Santa Monica, California, on November 13, 2003:

> FedEx, for example, has always emphasized great customer service, but now that we offer a broad array of services beyond just express delivery, we are seeking to differentiate ourselves through an outstanding customer experience, which is broader than just service. Not surprisingly we're taking the holistic approach. We want to make sure that the customer has a great experience at every touchpoint—on the phone with our service reps, on the web site while trying to ship a package, at the front door when our courier delivers the package and at our service centers when dropping off a package. And not only do we look at the touchpoints, but we also pay attention to the life cycle of the customer's experience. We try to treat the customer royally, not only when we first get her business, but also when her business needs or package volume change (Birla, 2005: 93).

This is the difference between focusing on efficiency versus effectiveness. An excuseless culture takes vision combined with values, not poring over output-input tables. It is more than just doing things right, it is about doing right by the customer.

Next, we will view the approach various firms have used to develop their own KPIs.

11

DEVELOPING KPIS FOR YOUR COMPANY

*Everything should be made as simple
as possible, but not simpler.*

—Albert Einstein

Developing KPIs is a metastrategy—that is, a strategy for defining strategies. They need to be intimately linked with the company's value proposition, as well as quantitative measurements, or—and this is even more important in knowledge companies—qualitative judgments. They should have a common definition and be understood across the entire organization, with no ambiguity, similar to the Continental and FedEx examples from Chapter 10.

They also have to be testable theories, in accordance with the scientific method discussed in Chapter 8. Recall the cyclical process of constructing a theory:

Observation

Categorization

Prediction

Confirmation

Having your entire team focused on KPIs not only gets the right job done daily, it also gives them a sense of commitment to the process of improving *how* that job gets done. Since the front lines are at the coal face, observing actual customer behavior, they know which processes work and which cause frustration, and can readily suggest improvements to make the customer experience more enjoyable. This process must be based on observed reality, and it must make sense in explaining *actual* customer behavior, not illusions or specious conclusions, as in the following story:

A scientist has two large jars before him, one containing many fleas, the other empty. He gently removes a flea from the flea jar, places it on the table before the empty jar, steps back, and commands, "Jump," whereupon the flea jumps into the empty jar. Methodically he gently removes each flea, places it on the table, says "Jump," and the flea jumps into the originally empty jar.

When he has transferred all the fleas in this way, he removes one from the now full jar, carefully pulls off its back legs, and places it on the table before the original jar. He commands, "Jump," but the flea does not move. He takes another flea from the jar, carefully pulls off its back legs, and places it on the table. Again he commands "Jump," but the flea does not move. Methodically he goes through this same procedure with the remaining fleas, and gets the same results. The scientist beamingly records in his notebook: "A flea when its back legs are pulled off, cannot hear" (Paulos, 2000: 129–30).

British philosopher Alfred North Whitehead defined the *fallacy of misplaced concreteness*—the mistake of confusing the manifestation of something with the thing itself. Every doctor knows a fever is not a disease, but merely a manifestation of one, and it is important to diagnose and treat the disease, not just the fever. A golfer does not have a scratch handicap, she swings the club, and if she does so with enough skill, a scratch handicap will be the result.

It is the same with profit: it is a lagging indicator of customer behavior. The points of the Continental Airlines and FedEx examples from Chapter 10 are important and go to the heart of what a company should measure. Who would suggest customers define the success of the businesses they patronize by how much profit it makes? There appears to be a gap between what leaders want their team members to do and what the customer wants them to do.

Before we can measure, we must first understand. Since it is important to recall how customers define the success—and failure—of the companies they do business with, Fred Smith's Hierarchy of Horrors exercise is a good place to start when developing KPIs, by studying customer complaints. Excellent customer service companies have service recovery strategies in place for the purpose of constantly improving the customer experience. Marriott hotels teaches the acronym LEARN—listen, empathize, apologize, react, and notify—to its team members so they know how to deal quickly and effectively with customer complaints. Each complaint is recorded to ensure the customer was satisfied, and for analysis on ways to reduce the future incident of the same issue affecting another customer.

The Ritz-Carlton has its famous Basics, which are 20 processes each employee is responsible for in carrying out the company's value statement: "We Are Ladies and Gentlemen Serving Ladies and Gentlemen." It also gives its team members great latitude in resolving customer complaints, with each one authorized to spend $2,000 on solving customer problems. In the Ritz-Carlton Basics, number 13 states: "Never lose a guest. Instant guest pacification is the responsibility of each employee. Whoever receives a complaint will own it, resolve it to the guest's satisfaction and record it." This "ownership" of customer complaints is quite effective, and a record over time will document many opportunities for developing your customer service canaries.

Providing a money-back service guarantee is another method for rewarding a customer to complain, so the organization can rectify the underlying service problems; and it even provides the opportunity to increase customer loyalty when the complaint is resolved to the customer's satisfaction.

Let us apply this method of analyzing complaints and compliments to a professional service firm, such as a law or accounting firm, and see which KPIs may make sense in that environment.

KPIS FOR A PROFESSIONAL SERVICE FIRM

Many studies have been done on why professionals lose and gain customers. Here are the results of three such studies, the first two on why CPAs lose and get customers, but the same could be said for doctors:

1. "My accountant just doesn't treat me right." [Two-thirds of the responses]
2. CPAs ignore clients.
3. CPAs fail to cooperate.
4. CPAs let partner contact lapse.
5. CPAs do not keep clients informed.
6. CPAs assume clients are technicians.
7. CPAs use clients as a training ground [for new team members].

    (Aquila and Koltin, 1992: 67–70)

And why people select accountants:

- Interpersonal skills
- Aggressiveness
- Interest in the customer
- Ability to explain procedures in terms the customer can understand
- Willingness to give advice
- Perceived honesty

    (Winston, 1995: 170)

David Maister, Charles H. Green, and Robert M. Galford, in *The Trusted Advisor,* offer the most commonly expressed customer suggestions regarding what they want from their professional relationship:

1. Make an impact on our business, don't just be visible.
2. Do more things "on spec" (i.e., invest your time on preliminary work in new areas).
3. Spend more time helping us think, and helping us develop strategies.
4. Lead our thinking. Tell us what our business is going to look like five or ten years from now.
5. *Jump* on any new pieces of information we have, so you can stay up-to-date on what's going on in our business. Use our data to give us an extra level of analysis. Ask for it, don't wait for us to give it to you.
6. Schedule some offsite meetings together. Join us for brainstorming sessions about our business.
7. Make an extra effort to understand how our business works: sit in on our meetings.
8. Help us see how we compare to others, both within and outside our industry.
9. Tell me why our competitors are doing what they're doing.
10. Discuss with us other things we should be doing; we welcome any and all ideas!

    (Maister, et. al., 2000: 180).

Despite all this evidence, the average professional service firm will track the hours its team members spend working on various assignments. There are many problems with this, the first being that no customer defines the success of their professionals by how many hours they spend on their work. It also focuses the team on efforts, activities, and inputs—not to mention ways to inflate their personal charge hours—at the expense of results, output, total quality service, and value to the customer. Another problem with this metric is that it is not a theory; and to add insult to injury, it is a lagging indicator. Perhaps this explains why the surveys mentioned on losing and gaining customers have not materially changed in the past half-century. The right measures, and judgments, are simply not on the dashboard of most professional service firms. The canaries are hacking and wheezing.

If a professional service firm wanted to develop leading KPIs, it should study the preceding factors to determine how it can create KPIs that would either discourage—or encourage—the behavior described. This requires modeling a theory of factors important to measure and reward, no small task for the professions. And in our experience with thousands of firms around the world, very few have taken the time to do this, let alone think about it.

Fortunately, this is beginning to change in some of the more enlightened firms. Our VeraSage Institute Team has been fortunate enough to conduct hundreds of workshops around the world on this very issue, and have had professionals from all categories brainstorm to come up with some KPIs for a professional service firm. We believe the following KPIs allow firms to eliminate timesheets, as they attempt to define success the same way the customer does. This provides the firm with a competitive advantage, which translates to enhanced pricing power.

Here are some firmwide KPIs selected by those firms who have quit using timesheets for a more customer-focused set of predictive indicators.

Firm-Wide KPIs—Velocity

- Turnaround Time

Firm-Wide KPIs—Financial

- Innovation sales

Firm-Wide KPIs—Customer

- Customer loyalty
- Share of customer wallet
- Value Gap
- Customer Referrals
- Number and quality of customer contacts per week

It is important to note there is ample evidence that between *three* to *five* KPIs should be enough for *any* business to have predictive value for customer behavior. Though I wanted to provide enough so you could at least begin to think in this direction—and perhaps develop even better KPIs for your particular company—it is important to keep in mind I am emphatically not suggesting you adopt *all* of the preceding KPIs. *Do not boil the ocean.* If you try to track too many KPIs, you end up knowing nothing, and would simply replace the timesheet measure with something even more burdensome.

Another caution: When choosing your firm's KPIs, do not overintellectualize the process. Selecting KPIs is not merely a matter of left-brain analysis; your firm's right brain is important, too. You are testing a theory, which will greatly influence what you are measuring and observing. You are looking for KPIs that will measure and reward results over activities, output over input, performance over methodology, responsibilities over procedures, and effectiveness over efficiency. The old joke among physicians applies here, where the surgeon is admiring his competence: "The operation was a complete success! Although the patient died, we kept him in perfect electrolyte balance throughout!"

Let us analyze each of the firmwide KPIs given, explain their logic, the results they are trying to measure, the behavior they are trying to encourage, how some professional service firms have implemented them, and even improved upon how they can be used to enhance a customer's experience in dealing with his or her professional. It should be noted that not all of the following KPIs are leading, some are coincident, and some may even be lagging, depending on how often they are disseminated throughout the organization.

Turnaround Time

Michael Dell likes to refer to the time lag between a customer placing an order and the company assembling and shipping the finished product as *velocity*. We believe professional service firms should also be diligent about tracking when each project comes in, establishing a desired completion date, and measuring the percentage of on-time delivery. This prevents procrastination, missed deadlines, and projects lingering in the firm while the customer is kept in the dark.

Borrowing Fred Smith's philosophy of creating an *excuseless culture*, imagine installing 360-degree webcams everywhere in a firm. Also imagine customers being able to log on to a secure Web site, type in their names and passwords, and the appropriate webcamera would find their project and give them a real-time picture of it, probably laying on a manager's floor or credenza awaiting review. Would this change the way work moved through a firm? Would this hold the firm accountable for results, not merely efforts? FedEx and UPS do exactly this; and, in fact, some of the larger law firms utilize intranets that provide their customers with real-time access to the work being performed on their behalf. Even some daycare facilities have installed webcams so parents can watch their child(ren) over the Internet while at work. Construction companies have done the same by installing webcams on job sites. This one metric would go a long way to solving most of the reasons customers defect from firms (not kept informed, feel ignored, and so on).

The turnaround KPI also implements Peter Drucker's recipe for avoiding the pitfalls of procrastination, by implementing the following alliterative triad of steps:

Definition, delegation, and deadline. The executive needed to define the problem or the task, delegate accountability to a specific person along with responsibility for the specific thing to be accomplished, and establish a firm deadline for completion. The definition ensured a sense of purpose, the delegation identified who was going to do the actual work, and the deadline substituted action for inertia (Flaherty, 1999: 328).

Turnaround time can be tracked at the firmwide level as well as the team member level (we will deal with team member KPIs in Chapter 12). If a particular team member is missing deadlines, it is a good indication he or she has been given too much work, does not have adequate training to do what has been assigned, is unclear on the assignment responsibilities, or is simply not up to the job. Whichever the reason, the turnaround time provides a leading indicator to firm executives to intervene and correct any problems in real time. The timesheet does not provide this advantage, because once it has been discovered, the problems are history.

Innovation Sales

This metric measures revenue from services introduced in recent years, and the firm's innovation in offering additional services to its customers. It is an essential measurement to determine the lifetime value of the firm to the customer. For example, Hewlett-Packard wants 50 percent of its revenue from products that did not exist two years ago. Intel achieves 100 percent of its revenues from products developed within the last three years. 3M targets 30 percent from products that did not exist four years ago.

Firms spend an enormous amount of resources measuring billable hours, realization rates, and other internal metrics, but we have found very few that measure innovation sales and make it a key component of its strategic vision. This is not to say firms are anti-innovation; it is more a matter of not being proinnovation, by not having measurements and reward systems in place to encourage this behavior. Innovation is essential to creating new wealth; as Gary Hamel asks, "What does it matter to an investor if a company is earning its cost of capital if its rivals are capturing the lion's share of new wealth in an industry?" (Hamel, 2000: 285).

Customer Loyalty

Frederick Reichheld, in his work with Bain & Company, estimated that fewer than 20 percent of corporate leaders rigorously track customer retention. For professional service firms, which derive anywhere from 80 to 95 percent of their revenue from existing customers, this is a major oversight. Also, when you consider it costs an average of 4 to 11 times more to *acquire* a customer than to *retain* one, this metric must become part of the firm's value system.

Share of Customer Wallet

This changes the firm's focus from market share and revenue growth to *better* growth by increasing the percentage the firm derives from each customer's budget for professional services. To increase this share over time, the firm must be up front with all customers that share of wallet is an important part of their long-term relationship. Unless it has a strategic reason for doing so, the firm should not allow its customers to distribute its work among many firms. It should make it part of the expectation with each customer that it wants the lion's share of their work, over the long run. This ensures a deeper relationship, increased loyalty, higher switching costs, premium prices, and greater profitability.

Value Gap

This measurement attempts to expose the gap between how much the firm could be yielding from its customers compared to how much it actually is. It is an excellent way to reward cross-selling additional services, increase the lifetime value of the firm to the customer, and gain a larger percentage of the customer's wallet. Marriott International uses predictive analytics, similar to the FICO example from Chapter 9, through its Hotel Optimization program. Marriott has developed a revenue opportunity model, comparing actual revenues as a percentage of optimal prices that could have been charged. It attributes the narrowing of this gap, from 83 to 91 percent, to this analysis. What actions can your firm take to close the value gap?

Customer Referrals

Because word of mouth is the most effective way to acquire the right kind of customers, referrals from existing customers are a leading indicator that the firm is delighting its current customers. A firm has no business taking on new customers if its existing customers are not completely happy. Also, if the firm's leaders are interested in promoting rainmaking activities at all levels within the firm—and rewarding them commensurately—customer referrals can also demonstrate the firm is asking its existing customers for contacts they believe could derive the same benefits as they do from doing business with the firm.

Number and Quality of Customer Contacts Per Week

Since two-thirds of customers defect from firms because of perceived indifference, why not encourage all of the firm's team members to meet regularly with the customers they serve? This keeps the firm visible and in front of the customer; will lead to a higher wallet share, more referrals, and increased loyalty; and aid in the development of communication and listening skills of team members.

However, this KPI cannot be gamed just to achieve some arbitrary quota of contacts per week; it must also consist of *subjective* evaluations of the quality of each contact: what was discussed, the body language of the customer, additional services discovered, and a host of other *judgments* that are simply too oblique to be measured quantitatively, but are the true characteristics of providing a good experience for customers while demonstrating you care about them.

Unlike a mass market company with millions of customers, many professional service firms have the ability to learn which KPIs are important to an individual customer. Many firms are now tracking KPIs for each customer or groups of similar customers. They uncover the important KPIs by conducting a thorough interview on expectations before accepting them as customers. They ask questions such as the following, used by my colleague, Dan Morris, in his CPA firm Morris + D'Angelo:

- Why did you initiate this contact?
- Please list your most important service issues.
- What are your expectations from a CPA/advisor?
- Please state how you would define a "successful" relationship.
- What is your annual advisor budget?
- How often would you like to meet with your CPA/advisor?
- Do you expect your CPA/advisor to contact you unilaterally throughout the year?
- How quickly do you expect a "returned" telephone call?
- What is your expected turnaround time for preparation of reports received by us?
- How do you feel about filing for tax return extensions?
- Would you like to receive email-based tax and financial related information?
- How do you feel about being contacted by a firm member other than a partner?

These questions were developed to prevent (and encourage) the type of behavior that causes customers to defect (and select) CPA firms. Assembling this information up front allows Dan's firm to customize the service experience and decide how much capacity will be required for each customer, and communicates to the entire team how to proceed in order to exceed the customer's expectations. While this method may seem cumbersome for a company with thousands or millions of customers, there is a good probability that many customers share the same KPIs and could be grouped into segments to monitor performance.

For example, Harrah's Casino uses the following KPIs: share of wallet, percentage of customers cross-sold (i.e., revenue derived from two or more Harrah's properties), and customer loyalty measured by the percentage of customers ascended to the highest tier of its Total Rewards loyalty program (it maintains three levels of frequent customers: gold, platinum, and diamond). Harrah's attributes this loyalty program to increasing share of wallet from 36 to 43 percent over five years, resulting in tripled revenues.

As good as these KPIs are, however, they are still *coincident* indicators, not necessarily leading. It would be interesting to know which KPIs Harrah's monitors on an hourly basis in its properties, which ultimately lead to the success of the stated performance results. As a general rule, any KPI that requires information from financial statements—income statement, balance sheet, or statement of cash flows—is usually a lagging or, at most, coincident indicator. All leading indicators are theories derived from information not found on financial statements.

KPIs EQUAL CUSTOMER ACCOUNTABILITY

Men have become the tools of their tools.

—Henry David Thoreau

There is little doubt that what you measure defines how people work, especially if those measurements determine pay, promotions, and other career advancements. Most organizations, when they are guided at all by indicators, do not formulate a set of coherent KPIs focused on the real-time, day-to-day, customer experience. Most performance measures are simply abstracted from lagging accounting data, and while they may be able to report the score of the game, they provide no insight or guidance on how to improve performance.

It may be worse than this. According to a Harris Interactive poll of 23,000 U.S. residents employed full-time within key industries and functional areas of firms, known as the xQ (Execution Quotient) Questionnaire, some key findings were:

- Only 37 percent said they have a clear understanding of what their organization is trying to achieve and why.
- Only 10 percent felt that their organization holds people accountable for results.
- Only 10 percent felt success measures are tracked adequately and openly.
- Only 10 percent felt people have clear, measurable, deadline-driven work goals.
- Only 20 percent fully trusted the organization they work for.
- Only 13 percent have high-trust, highly cooperative working relationships with other groups or departments (quoted in Covey, 2004: 2–3; 370–71).

This is the equivalent of coal miners descending into the mines without their canaries, not to mention lacking the understanding of what, exactly, their objectives are. Most people simply are not inspired to achieve the type of financial performance measurements dictated by the profit-and-loss statement. It is not inspiring to work somewhere simply to make "profits."

The genius of Fred Smith's concept of an excuseless culture at FedEx is that it holds all of the company's employees accountable to the customer, not simply their bosses or lagging financial metrics. By focusing on better serving its customers, FedEx is able to tap into discretionary team member energy, extending beyond simply performing the minimum requirements of their job. It also fosters creativity and innovation, as team members are engaged to find better ways to get their jobs done and create a better customer experience.

We have examined creating KPIs at a companywide level, those with predictive capability to peer into the future of customer behavior. It is time to cascade these companywide KPIs down deeper into the organization, at the individual team member level to align their day-to-day activities with the company's overall strategy, value, and mission. As W. Edward Demming used to say, "No organization can survive with just good people. They need people that are improving." In today's organizations, dominated as they are by knowledge workers, we need new metrics and models and new ways to think about how to increase the effectiveness of this ever increasing segment of the labor force.

12

INCREASING KNOWLEDGE WORKER EFFECTIVENESS

The single greatest challenge facing managers in the developed countries of the world is to raise the productivity of knowledge and service workers. This challenge, which will dominate the management agenda for the next several decades, will ultimately determine the competitive performance of companies. Even more important, it will determine the very fabric of society and the quality of life in every industrialized nation.

—Peter Drucker, *Peter Drucker on the Profession of Management,* 2003

What would you conclude regarding the productivity—that is, output divided by input—of a particular laser beam that wasted 60 to 90 percent of the electric power received at its back end before projecting an intense, blinding beam out the front?

It doesn't sound very efficient does it? Yet that is exactly the productivity of the laser beam used for cataract surgery to restore eyesight. It is not at all efficient. So what? It is highly effective. In this case, the waste of energy is clearly a virtue, not a vice. You would never draw this conclusion studying the ratio of output to input, however, as the math misses the miracle of restoring the joy of human sight. If you were the patient, inefficiency is clearly preferable to ineffectiveness.

This, in a nutshell, is the problem with the way we attempt to measure the "productivity" of knowledge workers. The metrics we are using are redolent of the days of Frederick Taylor, no longer applicable to the product of the intellect. Knowledge work is not repetitive, it is *iterative* and *reiterative.* That is, it is a process of the mind, a difficult place for metrics to have any meaning. Not many people would want a time-and-motion doctor, who equated efficiency with quality medical care.

The task at hand is formidable, since the relationship between inputs and outputs is not as well defined in the knowledge era as it was in the agricultural or industrial revolutions. Thus, the goal is not to shun Frederick Taylor, but to learn from him. Specifically, he applied knowledge to knowledge, increasing the productivity of manual laborers around the world, in the same manner Adam Smith explained the specialization and division of labor. However, even some of Smith's insights are not effective in a knowledge environment, since, for example, Shakespeare could not specialize in writing the verbs while a colleague wrote the nouns of his many works.

It does no good to admonish your team members to work *smarter* not *harder.* It's not bad advice, it's just not very helpful—like telling people to be healthy, wealthy, and wise. We need to apply the same ingenuity and creativity Taylor did to the subject of manual workers to increase the effectiveness of knowledge workers. To make progress on this ambition, we need to begin with a lesson from Plato: "The beginning of wisdom is the definition of terms."

WHAT, EXACTLY, IS PRODUCTIVITY?

Productivity is always a ratio, expressed as the amount of output per unit of input. Mathematically, it seems straightforward, as if there were one widely agreed on definition of the components of the numerator and denominator. In an intellectual capital economy, however, it is a conundrum. One of the most common measurements is output per man-hour, which in the United States has increased at an annual average rate of 3 percent since 1996. But this only measures labor productivity. Economists also measure multifactor productivity (or total factor productivity), which is an attempt to capture inputs beyond labor, such as capital. Yet, it is much easier to tally up hours worked than the value of capital, especially human capital.

The government measures most outputs by the cost of the inputs, hence it misses the prodigious growth of technology and other gains in knowledge, especially since the price of technology is constantly declining. This is exactly the quandary that led Nobel Laureate Robert Solow to utter, in 1987, "We see the computer age everywhere except in the productivity statistics."

In fact, according to a study by the McKinsey Global Institute, six sectors of the U.S. economy—comprising no more than 30 percent of its output—accounted for 99 percent of the increase in productivity between 1995 and 1999: retail, wholesale, securities, telecommunications, semiconductors, and computer manufacturing. The study attributed 23 percent of the productivity to Wal-Mart alone, and another 46 percent to its competitors racing to catch up (Gersemann, 2004: 35). Perhaps part of the explanation for productivity growth of less than 30 percent of the economy is that the measurements are inadequate and miss much of the intangible value of both the denominator and the numerator.

Take the denominator in the ratio. Which inputs should be included? If we are dealing with wine, we could count the grapes, the bottles, corks, and so on. But none of those would help us define—let alone value—the final product. As they say, it is much easier to count the bottles than describe the wine.

If we were dealing with Rembrandt's productivity, we could sum up the costs of paint, canvas, brushes, and even the amount of labor hours he spent plying his craft. Would there be any relationship to the final value of the output? Would counting the number of paintings produced over a given time period help? Companies have learned that costs are easier to compute than benefits, so they cut the costs in the denominator to improve the efficiency. This is the equivalent of Walt Disney cutting out three of the dwarfs in *Snow White and the Seven Dwarfs* in order to reduce the inputs, making the resulting ratio look better. Efficient, yes; effective, hardly.

Obviously, the denominator cannot go below zero, but the numerator can be practically infinite—witness Bill Gates or the founders of Google. The output side of the ratio includes intangibles such as innovation, quality customer service, brand value, passion, and other traits next to impossible to quantify. Consider this letter from a very happy Walt Disney World guest:

> My family and I went to Walt Disney World a few years ago. I purchased an autograph book and put my name and address inside the front cover, but as luck would have it, I lost it before I was able to get any signatures. Six months later, I received a package from Walt Disney World. Inside was my book, filled with autographs from every Disney character you could imagine, and a signed picture of all the characters in front of Cinderella Castle!
>
> —*Kristie Gardner*
> *Glenwood, New Jersey*
> (*Disney Magazine,*
> Winter 2004–2005: 11)

Certainly, the cost of the actions by Disney employees in this incident can be calculated, but what about the intangible goodwill created? Taking actions such as this can even make efficiency look worse, because our metrics are simply not sophisticated enough to capture the value of the outputs. We can calculate how many surgeries the cardiologist performs, but it doesn't tell us anything about the quality of life for his or her patients.

The fact of the matter is, we do not know how to measure the productivity of a knowledge worker. And even if we someday figure it out, we have not won even half the battle. We would still need to know how to increase it. Ignorance may be postponed knowledge, as David Hume said; but in this case, it extends not only to the monumental productivity calculation, but to the very definition—and number—of knowledge workers.

HOW MANY KNOWLEDGE WORKERS ARE THERE?

This is probably a trivial question, since knowing the number of knowledge workers in the labor force sheds no light on how to increase their effectiveness. It does, however, give us a vector on how the economy has shifted from an industrial base to a knowledge base.

Since the United States Bureau of Labor Statistics does not yet classify knowledge workers separately, one needs to make judgments about which type of occupations to include. Several attempts have been made, one of them by author and consultant Thomas Davenport, whose definition of knowledge workers includes the following occupations: management; business and financial operations; computer technology and mathematics; architecture and engineering; life, physical, and social sciences; legal and healthcare practices; community and social services, education, training, and library science; arts, design, entertainment, sports; and the media. This totals some 36 million workers, or approximately 28 percent of the labor force (Davenport, 2005: 5).

Richard Florida, a nonresident senior fellow at the Brookings Institution and Hirst Professor at George Mason University's School of Public Policy, uses a different term than knowledge worker, preferring instead "creative class." He describes the rise of this segment of labor force in his books, *The Rise of the Creative Class* (2002), and *The Flight of the Creative Class,* the latter in which he puts the number at almost 40 million Americans, or 30 percent of all those employed (Florida, 2005: 28).

Florida estimates that approximately 10 percent of the U.S. workforce were in this sector in 1900, growing to 20 percent in 1980; today, they exceed the number of traditional blue-collar workers. This trend is similar in all of the industrialized nations. Florida includes workers in science and engineering; architecture and design; education, arts, music, and entertainment; and anyone else "whose economic function is to create new ideas, new technology and/or new creative content." This would also include a "broader group of *creative professionals* in business and finance, law, health care and related fields" (Florida, 2002: 8). Florida estimates workers in the service sector at roughly 55 million, or 45 percent of the workforce (ibid: 9).

But no matter how many of them exist, the number of knowledge workers is growing twice as fast as in other segments of the labor force; furthermore, they are the highest paid and comprise the lion's share of the value—and wealth-producing capacity—of today's companies. Increasing their effectiveness is, therefore, a worthwhile and important task of today's leaders.

A FRAMEWORK FOR KNOWLEDGE WORKER EFFECTIVENESS

What made the traditional workforce productive was the system—whether it was Frederick Winslow Taylor's "one best way," Henry Ford's assembly line, or Ed Demming's Total Quality Management. The system embodies the knowledge. The system is productive because it enables individual workers to perform without much knowledge or skill. . . . In a knowledge-based organization, however, it is the individual worker's productivity that makes the system productive. In a traditional workforce, the worker serves the system; in a knowledge workforce, the system must serve the worker.

—Peter Drucker, *Managing in the Next Society,* 2002

Knowledge work is not defined so much by *quantity* as it is by *quality.* It is also not defined by its *costs* but by its *results.* Frederick Taylor started with the assumption that there was "one best way" to achieve productivity and it was not necessarily determined by the physical—or even mental—characteristics of the job. But in knowledge work, the traditional tools of measurement need to be replaced by *judgment,* and there is a difference between a measurement and a judgment: a measurement requires only a stick; a judgment requires knowledge.

Frederick Taylor did not attempt to measure the productivity of knowledge workers because there were not very many in his day. He did not focus attention on how to train the workers to do the job better next time, because he developed systems and procedures that removed the need for them to use their imaginations. He substituted rules for thinking.

It took approximately a half-century before companies began to learn this made their organizations complacent and stupid—not the traits you want in an auto factory, let alone among knowledge workers. Knowledge work can only be designed *by* the knowledge worker, not *for* the worker. In a factory, the worker *serves* the system. The same is true in a *service* environment; but in a knowledge environment, the system should *serve* the worker.

In fact, the term *service worker* was coined around 1920, when fewer than half of all nonmanual workers were actually employed in service jobs— such as banking, insurance, restaurants, government, and so on. The same metrics were applied to these industries as Taylor did to factory workers, and they were accurate enough at establishing a relationship between inputs and outputs. The terms *knowledge industries, knowledge work,* and *knowledge worker* are only 45 years old. They were coined around 1961, simultaneously but independently, the first by a Princeton economist, Fritz Machlup, the second and third by Peter Drucker.

We need new thinking and new models to *judge* the effectiveness of knowledge workers. Fortunately, Peter Drucker blazed the trail in this area, a modern-day Taylor for the knowledge worker. Wise executives will build on his wisdom to usher in the new era of the knowledge worker.

Productivity measurements on knowledge work may be in their infancy, but Drucker has left us a good starting place, especially in his book *Management Challenges for the 21st Century*:

> Work on the productivity of the knowledge worker has barely begun. In terms of actual work on knowledge worker productivity, we are, in the year 2000, roughly where we were in the year 1900, a century ago, in terms of the productivity of the manual worker. But we already know infinitely more about the productivity of the knowledge worker than we did then about that of the manual worker. We even know a good many of the answers. But we also know the challenges to which we do not yet know the answers, and on which we need to go to work. *Six* major factors determine knowledge-worker productivity.
>
> 1. Knowledge-worker productivity demands that we ask the question: *"What is the task?"*
>
> 2. It demands that we impose the responsibility for their productivity on the individual knowledge workers themselves. Knowledge workers *have* to manage themselves. They have to have *autonomy.*
>
> 3. Continuing innovation has to be part of the work, the task and the responsibility of knowledge workers.
>
> 4. Knowledge work requires continuous learning on the part of the knowledge worker, but equally continuous teaching on the part of the knowledge worker.

5. Productivity of the knowledge worker is not—at least not primarily—a matter of the *quantity* of output. *Quality* is at least as important [I would argue, more important].

6. Finally, knowledge-worker productivity requires that the knowledge worker is both seen and treated as an "asset" [I would say, volunteer] rather than a "cost." It requires that knowledge workers *want* to work for the organization in preference to all other opportunities (Drucker, 1999: 142).

These factors are almost the exact opposite of what is needed to increase the productivity of manual labor, with the possible exception of number six. The word "manufacturing" is derived from *manufactory,* meaning "made by hand." Yet more and more of today's economic output is made by mind. Taylor's systems did not engage the mind; they actually were designed to disengage it, similar to flying an airplane on autopilot.

Drucker believed the main focus of the knowledge worker needs to be on the task to be done—with all other distractions eliminated as much as possible—and this is defined by the worker him- or herself. Asking knowledge workers the following questions (adapted from Peter Drucker and other sources) about their jobs is a rich source of learning a great deal about any organization:

- What is your task?
- What should it be?
- What should you be expected to contribute?
- How fair are those expectations?
- What hampers you in doing your task and should be eliminated?
- How could *you* make the greatest *contribution* with your strengths, your way of performing, your values, to what needs to be done?
- What *results* have to be achieved to make a difference?
- What hinders you in doing your task and should be eliminated?
- What progress are you making in your career?
- How is the company helping you to achieve your professional goals and aspirations?
- What does the company do right and what should it continue doing?
- What are the firm's weaknesses and what should it stop doing?
- What critical things should the firm start doing?

These are excellent questions for executives to ask their team members periodically. Between the preceding KPIs and these questions, the firm will be able to focus its resources and attention on external opportunities, rather than on internal bureaucratic procedures, rules, and systems that probably do not add much value to the customer experience.

Recall that a business does not exist to be efficient; it exists to create wealth for its customers. The traditional focus on efficiency in an intellectual-capital-based economy is misplaced. This is not to say that productivity is not important, rather that it should not be the talisman for guiding the company to its core purpose: the creation of wealth.

Efficiency can be taken to ludicrous extremes. For instance, I doubt any efficiency expert would have suggested to the Nordstrom brothers to place pianos and hire piano players in their department stores. What could this possibly add to efficiency? Yet, how *effective* is it in providing a competitive differentiation that Nordstrom can leverage to create a more valuable experience for its team members and customers?

Knowledge companies understand this dynamic. Disney and Apple know there is a vast difference between being efficient and being *persuasive.* Gordon Bethune saw first-hand the pernicious effects of focusing on nothing but costs when he took over the helm at Continental Airlines. Even Ben & Jerry's understood that a business simply could not operate at—or price for—100 percent efficiency. The new companies that have created so much wealth in the past decades, from eBay and Intel to Starbucks, Microsoft, and Google, did not get where they are by focusing on efficiency. They focused on creating wealth for their customers. Why, then, do so many companies worship on the altar of efficiency, confusing being busy with being profitable?

It is time to replace efficiency with *effectiveness,* and begin to measure what counts, rather than counting for the sake of counting. Frederick Taylor's time-and-motion studies have no place in the business of the future because it is not an accurate measurement of the *results* and *wealth* knowledge workers create for their customers. We need KPIs for knowledge workers that create an environment of responsible autonomy, where workers will decide for themselves what and how to perform their jobs, while taking full responsibility and accountability for the outcome.

KEY PREDICTIVE INDICATORS FOR KNOWLEDGE WORKERS

I'd rather be vaguely right than precisely wrong.

—John Maynard Keynes

Alvin Toffler used to confound business audiences by asking what it would cost them if none of their employees had ever been toilet-trained. This human capital is an enormous subsidy provided to society but it defies any meaningful measurement. It is much the same situation in trying to develop measurements for knowledge workers—humans simply cannot be measured and managed by numbers alone.

Many of the "hard" and "objective" measures we do use can be gotten around with a modicum of intelligence by the average worker. It is actually the "soft," "fuzzy," and "subjective" measures that are harder for executives to deal with, because they require judgment and discernment. Measurements only require a scale, and it is much easier to be precisely irrelevant than it is to be approximately relevant. Measures also provide us with the illusion of precise control, as if you could manage people by managing numbers. I'd rather be vaguely right about a soft measure than precisely wrong about a hard measure.

The following knowledge worker KPIs are offered in the spirit of flouting bureaucratic command-and-control rules in order to direct performance from an externally guided standard, all the while maintaining a sense of pride in helping others, which is one of the most important intrinsic rewards people earn from their careers.

Customer Feedback

What are the customers saying—good and bad—about the team member? Would you trade some efficiency for a team member who was absolutely loved by your customers? How does the firm solicit feedback from its customers on team member performance? Does the firm reward team members for delivering outstanding customer service or going above and beyond the call of duty for a customer? Are these stories shared with the rest of the company so they can become part of its culture, as they are at Nordstrom, Southwest, FedEx, and Disney?

Effective Listening and Communication Skills

If reading and writing go together, so too do speaking and listening. Yet is anyone really ever taught to listen? It is well known that speaking and listening are harder to teach than reading and writing; and if we lament the low level of reading and writing being taught in the schools, just think how much less developed speaking and listening skills must be. Unlike reading and writing, which are solitary undertakings, listening and speaking always involve human interactions.

Aristotle's book, *Rhetoric,* explained the art of persuasion by using the three Greek words: *ethos, pathos,* and *logos.* Ethos signifies a person's character, the sense that you can be trusted and know what you are talking about. Pathos is arousing the passions of the listeners, getting their emotions running in the direction you are trying to take them. It is the motivating factor. Logos is the intellectual reason—and note the Greeks put it last. Think of the old saying, "People do not care how much you know until they know how much you care." Reasons and arguments can be used to reinforce your position, but it is the passion that will move the listeners in your direction.

But how do you measure listening and communication skills? It is truly a soft measure, but is it not a critical skill for the development of a true knowledge worker, especially in an era where teamwork and wide collaboration with others is essential to perform their tasks? I once observed a panel discussion at the American Institute of Certified Public Accountant's Group 100 meeting of executives in corporations and government agencies that hire CPAs, lawyers, and consultants. The number-one capability they look for—and it influences their decision to hire one firm over another, before price or quality—is communication skills. Organizations need to invest in the education necessary to make their team members exceptional in these skills.

Risk Taking, Innovation, and Creativity

These are other soft measures, but critical skills for any knowledge worker. How often do they take risks or innovate new ways of doing things for customers or the company? Do they engage in creative thinking in approaching their work? Most executives say they want their people to "think out of the box," but when you look at what they measure and reward there is an enormous gap between what they say and what they do.

Innovation and creativity need not be thought of as separate from the rest of the business, but rather an integral part of it. Shouldn't firms work to make innovation ordinary, as the example of FedEx leveraging the ideas of all of its employees in order to do the job better demonstrates?

This is precisely why 3M implemented the "15 percent rule," which encourages technical people to spend up to 15 percent of their time on projects of their own choosing and initiative. W.L. Gore, a $1.35 billion company with 6,000 employees, allows 10 percent free time to dream up new applications for the company's materials.

Both companies use milestones and subjective evaluations to determine progress, not financial numbers, which are of little use in determining the success or failure of various R&D products, or start-up ventures. I am met with "staring ovations" when I suggest knowledge firms adopt a similar policy, where at least the knowledge workers are given time to dream up better ways to innovate, improve systems, or add value to customers. As Ikujiro Nonaka and Hirotaka Takeuchi say in *The Knowledge-Creating Company,* "Allow employees time to pursue harebrained schemes or just sit around chatting, and you may come up with a market-changing idea; force them to account for every minute of their day, and you will be stuck with routine products." It was this very policy that led to the development of the Post-it Note, where an incredible amount of wealth was created in this new market for the small price of less efficiency.

Knowledge Elicitation

Ross Dawson, in his book *Developing Knowledge-Based Client Relationships: The Future of Professional Services,* describes knowledge elicitation as "the process of assisting others to generate their own knowledge." Note that this encompasses more than simply learning new things; it involves educating others so they generate their own knowledge. One of the most effective techniques for knowledge workers to learn any subject—especially at a very deep level—is to teach it. As they say, to teach is to learn twice. How often do the team members facilitate a lunch and learn from an article or book they have read or seminar they have attended? How good are they at educating their customers?

Effective Knowledge Producer and Consumer

This KPI is designed to measure how well the team members draw from—and contribute to—the company's intellectual capital. Are they simply consumers of IC or do they also produce IC? How many after-action reviews (AARs) have they written up? (Note: AARs were explained in *Pricing on Purpose,* and will be expanded upon in the next book in the Intellectual Capitalism Series). How many times were those AARs accessed by other members of the firm? How well do they convert their *tacit* knowledge into *explicit* knowledge the firm can reuse and make part of its structural capital? Do they look for the most effective way to leverage knowledge, or do they merely reinvent the wheel? This type of evaluation will help ensure the firm is leveraging what really counts—its IC—and developing more of it.

Ability to Deal with Change

How well do the team members adapt to discontinuity, ambiguity, and tumultuous change? How do they assist others—colleagues and customers alike—in dealing with change? Sure, this is another soft skill, but a critical one in developing the type of temperament required to become a successful knowledge worker.

Continuous Learning

What do team members know this year that they did not know last year that makes them more valuable to the firm and its customers? This is more than simply logging time in educational courses; it would actually require an attempt to assess what they learned. Are they constantly enhancing their skills to become more effective workers? How many books have they read this year? More important, what did they learn from them? Does the firm adequately invest in its people's education in order to fulfill this mission? An awful lot, it seems, do not, and the majority of team members are starved for life-long education, and will gravitate to those firms that offer it.

Effective Delegator

Peter Drucker wrote: "I have yet to see a knowledge worker, regardless of rank or station, who could not consign something like a quarter of the demands on his time to the wastepaper basket without anybody's noticing their disappearance" (Drucker, 2006: 17). If true—and I suspect it is, although I know of no empirical study that confirms it—this is an astonishing figure. Think of the additional leverage your firm would gain if its senior team members were able and willing to delegate up to 25 percent of their work. Not only would it provide needed skills for junior team members, it would make available greater capacity to service first-class and business-class customers with more valuable projects, the true specialization advantage of the knowledge worker. If the firm's knowledge workers were to become better at delegation, it would increase profitability many times more than an increase in efficiency could ever provide. Does your firm encourage its knowledge workers to become effective delegators, as opposed to hoarding work to meet irrelevant performance evaluations? It is worth thinking about.

Mentoring and Coaching Skills

How well does the firm develop team members who can coach and mentor those less experienced? Are adequate resources being invested in this area? I have seen my share of mentoring programs fail, or deliver lackluster results, and remain unconvinced of their worthiness. Perhaps the reason is that a mentor cannot be thrust upon someone; rather, it is a voluntary relationship that develops over time. But this does not preclude it from happening within the firm. Knowledge workers cannot be managed—even Peter Drucker thought the word manager was becoming obsolete, and should be replaced by executive. They can, though, be coached, motivated, directed, focused, and inspired to perform based upon their strengths. Even Tiger Woods is coached, and the best players are not necessarily the best coaches.

Personal Development

What inspires knowledge workers? Why did they enter their chosen careers —or your company—in the first place? What is their preferred vision of the future? How is the firm helping—or hindering—their professional development? These are all vital areas to address if you intend to retain and develop your human capital investors, who are, ultimately, volunteers.

Pride

I agree with Jon Katzenbach, coauthor of *The Wisdom of Teams*:

> Pride is a more effective motivator of a professional's talent than money. And you can motivate that talent with pride in more than just belonging. There is pride in the specific work product that you deliver to clients, pride in the kinds of clients that you serve, pride in the expertise that you can apply, pride in the values of your firm (quoted in McKenna and Maister, 2002: 147–48).

If you thought some of the preceding KPIs were hard to measure, how would you measure pride? Yet it is obvious that pride in one's work, customers, colleagues, employer, and values are critical in order to operate with passion and commitment, the next KPI.

Passion, Attitude, and Commitment

These are perhaps the three most subjective criteria, none of which is a substitute for actual talent, but can there be any doubt that passion, attitude, and commitment are important to the effectiveness of a knowledge worker?

The glass can be either half empty or half full, depending on your disposition. Mathematically, these are the exact same positions, but in the arena of human decisions and actions, they lead to radically different consequences. For example, if you wanted to predict the risk of low birthrate among newborns, there are several factors you could posit, from the income of the mother, access to health care, or possessing health insurance. It turns out that none of these factors has explanatory power. The one that does is the mother's *attitude* toward her pregnancy, and that requires a *subjective* evaluation, not a measurement. As Homer Simpson explains to his daughter Lisa: "If adults don't like their jobs, they don't go on strike. They just go in every day and do it really half-assed."

High Satisfaction Day™

I am indebted to John Heymann, CEO, and his team at NewLevel Group, a consulting firm located in Napa, California (www.newlevelgroup.com), for this KPI. When John's firm held a retreat for the purpose of developing their KPIs, the suggestion of high satisfaction day (HSD) was made. An HSD is one of those days that convinces you, beyond doubt, why you do what you do. It could mean landing a new customer, achieving a breakthrough on an existing project, receiving a heartfelt thank-you from a customer, or any other emotion of exhilaration that makes you happy you got out of bed in the morning. Sound touchy-feely? John admits it is; but he also says the number of HSDs logged into the firm's calendar is a leading indicator—and a barometer—of his firm's morale.

Here is how John defined the effectiveness of this KPI in an e-mail to me on February 21, 2006:

> As for the HSD, it's really meant as a check for more than just "happiness." We have a well-defined culture and values that we believe, if nurtured, will yield exceptional results (we already have some bottom-line evidence of the effect). Our core values include commitment, collaboration and, especially, a focus on results. We find that the things that trigger an HSD generally stem from paying attention to those values. Therefore, the greater number of HSDs experienced, the stronger our culture becomes, leading to increased performance (results).
>
> Also, the commitment/collaboration values demand (and engender) a high-trust culture, and an HSD-type of metric draws attention to the individual's own drive and success without requiring a subjective management judgment, so it removes a lot of the frustration professionals often feel at having their performance judged by others. Smart people don't need to be controlled, they need to be in an environment where they feel valued and respected so they can make a difference while being successful. What's the old saw? If you have smart employees, your job is not to motivate them—it's to not demotivate them.
>
> I hope that helps clarify a bit more—I could go on! HSDs *are* touchy-feely, but I'm okay with that. Perhaps we need more insights into humanistic management practices instead of just the science. At [my old firm] people joked that my title stood for Chief Emotional Officer.

In a survey of 254 employers, titled "Job Outlook 2005," by the National Association of Colleges and Employers of Bethlehem, Pennsylvania, prospective employers said the most important qualities they look for are, on a scale of 1 to 5, from not important to extremely important:

Communication skills	4.7
Honesty and integrity	4.7
Relating and working well with others	4.5
Strong work ethic	4.5
Teamwork skills	4.5
Analytical skills	4.4
Motivation and initiative	4.4
Flexibility and adaptability	4.3
Computer skills	4.2
Detail-oriented	4.1
Leadership	4.0
Organizational skills	4.0

(www.naceweb.org, accessed February 16, 2006).

With the possible exceptions of analytical and computer skills, I defy anyone to *objectively* measure the preceding criteria. This is why hiring a knowledge worker is fraught with so much more risk than other types of employees. Once someone is assessed to have these traits, they are thrown into an environment where metric mania takes over and tries to quantify, count, and objectify everything they do. Formulas just cannot adequately deal with these critical characteristics of knowledge workers. To be sure, these criteria raise more questions than they answer, but at least they are the right questions.

KPI GUIDELINES

Selecting from the KPIs given here, or developing more appropriate ones of your own, should be done with the involvement of your team members. Although it is widely believed that people do not like change, there is a difference between change *imposed* and change *adopted*. As Michael Basch reminds us: "People don't mind change. They mind being changed."

Let the team members decide which KPIs they want to be held accountable for. These are smart, bright, motivated knowledge workers who want to do an outstanding job not only for the customers and the company, but also for themselves. They know what the key predictors of success are. The debate about organizational control is not whether it is needed—it certainly is— but about how it is best achieved. Imposing controls such as lagging financial metrics, which do not have a palpable relationship with customer success, might result in obedience and the minimum level of effort to obtain the standards, but it will not drive excellence. Of course, you will encounter resistance from those who are mired in measurements—the tail-less dog praises tail-lessness, according to the historian Collingwood—and feel threatened by KPIs that attempt to *judge* actual output and results. But so what? This is precisely the historically hysterical mind-set we are trying to change.

Organizations that have let the team select their own KPIs discovered, usually to their pleasant surprise, that they chose KPIs that were tougher on themselves than the executives would have been. People who select their own goals are usually more demanding of themselves than when those goals are selected for them.

Robert B. Cialdini, the Regents Professor of Psychology at Arizona State University, labels this "the Principle of Consistency." In his article titled "Harnessing the Science of Persuasion," in *Harvard Business Review,* he explains this principle:

> People align with their clear commitments. Make their commitments active, public, and voluntary. My own research has demonstrated that most people, once they take a stand or go on record in favor of a position, prefer to stick to it. . . . Israeli researchers writing in 1983 in the *Personality and Social Psychology Bulletin* recounted how they asked half the residents of a large apartment complex to sign a petition favoring the establishment of a recreation center for the handicapped. The cause was good and the request was small, so almost everyone who was asked agreed to sign. Two weeks later, on National Collection Day for the Handicapped, all residents of the complex were approached at home and asked to give to the cause. A little more than half of those who were not asked to sign the petition made a contribution. But an astounding 92 percent of those who did sign donated money. The residents of the apartment complex felt obligated to live up to their commitments because those commitments were active, public, and voluntary.
>
> More than 300 years ago, Samuel Butler wrote a couplet that explains succinctly why commitments must be voluntary to be lasting and effective: "He that complies against his will/Is of his own position still" (Cialdini, 2001: 76–77).

Social controls and trust are more effective than financial controls for influencing your team members' behavior. This explains why companies that have substituted traditional financial metrics with KPIs make them as transparent as possible. If you know your peers are holding you responsible and answerable for your activities, you are more likely to act in a manner consistent with the wishes of the group.

Another practical suggestion to hold people accountable for their contributions, when combined with the KPIs given here, is what Peter Drucker called the *manager's letter*:

> This [setting objectives] is so important that some of the most effective managers I know go one step further. They have each of their subordinates write a "manager's letter" twice a year. In this letter to his superior, each manager first defines the objectives of his superior's job and of his own job as he sees them. He then sets down the performance standards that he believes are being applied to him. Next, he lists the things he must do himself to attain these goals—and the things within his own unit he considers the major obstacles. He lists the things his superior and the company do that help him and the things that hamper him. Finally, he outlines what he proposes to do during the next year to reach his goals. If his superior accepts this statement, the "manager's letter" becomes the charter under which the manager operates (quoted in Flaherty, 1999: 93).

Implementing KPIs and the manager's letter suggested by Drucker requires enlightened leaders who understand that knowledge workers must contribute based on their strengths, and be given autonomy over how they do their work. This attitude does not fit well with the Taylorite command-and-control hierarchies, but it will become an essential mind-shift if we are to reap the rewards of knowledge workers.

Let us now join the debate raging among those who believe in *managing by results* versus those who are proponents of *managing by means*. There are valuable lessons to be learned from the teachings of each side, and the dissension needs to be encouraged as it will no doubt further our advancement of making today's knowledge workers more effective, rather than just more efficient—a worthy objective all can agree on.

13

MANAGING BY RESULTS VERSUS MANAGING BY MEANS

*Sometimes the numbers don't explain everything. The numbers
are not the business — they are symbols of the business.*

—Gerald Deitchle, Cheesecake's CFO

Imagine four friends getting together every Friday night to play poker. Over the course of a year, Player A wins 75 percent of the time; Player B, 15 percent; Player C, 5 percent; and Player D, 5 percent. Knowing these results with exact certitude, are you prepared to draw any conclusions regarding the outcome of the games?

We may be tempted to conclude Player A cheats, but we might also be tempted to surmise that Players B, C, and D have awful poker faces. In other words, looking at the *results* does not give us much indication of the *process* by which the games were played. For that, we would need to observe the games before making judgments.

This difference is the very essence of the debate between those who believe in what I am going to label "management by results," and others who advocate "management by means." The former claims its roots, somewhat erroneously, in the scientific method, while the latter draws on nature and biological analogies, describing businesses as interdependent systems that cannot be mechanistically manipulated, especially by measurements. This is such an important debate it is worth taking a historical detour to explore its origins.

FEUDING INTELLECTUALS: RESULTS VERSUS MEANS

In 1987, Professors H. Thomas Johnson and Robert S. Kaplan published *Relevance Lost: The Rise and Fall of Management Accounting,* which was named, in 1997, one of the 14 most influential management books to appear in the first 75 years of *Harvard Business Review's* history. The book is credited with launching the activity-based costing (ABC) revolution. Despite their historical collaboration, these two thinkers have gone down very different paths as of late. Kaplan is doing pioneering work in the field of the Balanced Scorecard, and Johnson is moving on to what he calls "management by means." In fact, they are now feuding with each other, and have not spoken in years.

I thought it would be beneficial to compare and contrast the approaches these two seminal thinkers advocate, since this debate is far from over, and will influence management thinking for decades to come.

Management by Results

In their classic 1992 *Harvard Business Review* article, "The Balanced Scorecard: Measures That Drive Performance," Robert S. Kaplan and David P. Norton asserted their case for the Balanced Scorecard approach, suggesting companies link their strategic goals to measures in four areas:

- Financial perspective
- Customer perspective
- Business process perspective
- Learning and growth perspective

Declaring "What you measure is what you get," they also pointed out how the traditional measures of the industrial era were no longer relevant to the type of organizations many companies were aspiring to become—that is, knowledge-based. They also acknowledged "no single measure can provide a clear performance target or focus attention on the critical areas of the business."

On the Web site www.balancedscorecard.org there is an example of measures used for a fictional airline, in each of the four areas just listed. Here are the KPIs suggested for each area, driven by the strategic mission of the airline: "Dedication to the highest quality of Customer Service delivered with a sense of warmth, friendliness, individual pride, and Company Spirit":

Area	Objectives	Measures
Financial	Profitability	Market value
	Fewer planes	Seat revenue
	Increase revenue	Plane lease cost
Customer	Flight on-time	FAA on-time rank
	Lowest prices	Customer ranking
	More customers	Number of customers

Area	Objectives	Measures
Internal	Fast ground turnaround	On-ground time On-time departure
Learning	Ground crew alignment	% ground crew stockholders % ground crew trained

Compare these KPIs to the three used by Gordon Bethune at Continental Airlines, as discussed in Chapter 10 (on-time arrival, lost luggage, customer complaints). Obviously, not all of these KPIs are going to be relevant hour by hour to each employee. Others are lagging indicators. Still, this is a superior approach to managing based solely on financial reports, because some of these KPIs do possess predictive capability.

Unfortunately, some companies have put together lengthy scorecards with a hodgepodge of indicators, many of which are lagging. Some consultants suggest upward of 25 KPIs, which is an attempt to boil the ocean. If the Balanced Scorecard is truly rooted in the scientific method, then surely many of the scorecards could benefit from a shave from Occam's razor. There is no such thing as a free statistic, as Jeffrey Pfeffer, the Thomas D. Dee Professor of Organizational Behavior at Stanford Graduate School of Business, explains in an interview in *Fast Company*:

> There's an old saying in business: What gets measured is what gets done. What's happening today is the flip side of that. Measurement has become a tyranny that makes sure that nothing gets done.
>
> I've developed what I like to call the Otis Redding Theory of Measurement, which is named for his song "Sittin' on the Dock of the Bay." In that song, Redding sings, "I can't do what 10 people tell me to do, so I guess I'll remain the same." That line sounds as if it could be about companies' misconceptions about measurement.
>
> Companies have managed to convince themselves that, since what gets measured is what gets done, the more they measure, the more stuff will get done. Last summer, I met a woman who works for a large oil company, and she told me that the company has 105 measures for which she is responsible. So I asked her, "How many of those 105 measures do you pay attention to?" Her answer? "None." Because in the end, she's measuring so many things that she doesn't pay attention to any of them—105 equals zero (www.fastcompany.com/online/35/pfeffer.html, June 2000).

Some of the criticisms leveled against the Balanced Scorecard approach are patently unfair. Kaplan and Norton were very cautious and realistic about its shortcomings, writing:

> Even the best objective can be achieved badly. . . . Even an excellent set of balanced scorecard measures does not guarantee a winning strategy.

The balanced scorecard can only translate a company's strategy into specific measurable objectives.

Senior managers may know what the end result should be, but they cannot tell employees exactly how to achieve that result, if only because the conditions in which employees operate are constantly changing (Kaplan and Norton, 2005: 174, 179, 180).

As with any tool, the Balanced Scorecard can be used well or badly, and the originators should not be held accountable for faulty implementation of their ideas. That being said, the jury is still out on the effectiveness of this approach. As anyone who has ever worked in an organization can tell you: "Hold me accountable for a specific measurement, and I'll figure out a way to game the system." This is the intrinsic beauty of human nature.

Gaming the Measurement System

[Workers] will likely meet the targets—even if they
have to destroy the enterprise to do it.

—W. Edwards Deming

There is an old medical school joke that asks: "What do you call a student who graduated hundredth out of a class of 100?" Answer: "Doctor." Without the context, this statistic is meaningless, as even the last-ranked student may still be a better doctor than all the other graduates from lesser-quality schools, or the alternative of no doctor at all. Even so, it is simply statistically impossible for everyone to have the top-ranked doctors.

Any measure is going to require judgment, otherwise manipulating numbers will become more important than creating value for customers. Consider the many ways clever people can improve on what is measured, especially if the focus is on quarterly results:

- Measuring on revenue per employee? We'll outsource what may be vital tasks, even at the expense of destroying customer value.
- Measuring time to market? We'll just make incremental, minor improvements to existing products.
- Measuring sales growth, or imposing revenue targets? We'll add unprofitable customers. (See my previous book, *Pricing on Purpose,* for a more in-depth discussion of the harmful effects of this practice and what to do about it.)
- Measuring number of patents filed? We'll simply bypass the internal review process and file any idea we can.

- Measuring our lagging evaluation scores as seminar leaders? We'll let people out early, serve cold milk and warm cookies, have their cars washed in the parking lot, and show movies.

Heisenberg's Uncertainty Principle applies to all measures: that the observer in a scientific experiment affects the result. Human ingenuity is not just found in for-profit organizations, but even in universities, as Andrew J. Policano, former dean of the University of Wisconsin-Madison, explains in his 2001 article "Ten Easy Steps to a Top-25 MBA Program":

> If your MBA program is in the unenviable group that *BusinessWeek* and *U.S. News & World Report* rank below the top 25, you are undoubtedly under constant pressure from your students, alumni, and donors to move into the top 25. The following . . . steps [among others] can get you there. . . .
>
> - *Provide a wide variety of students' services for MBA students,* including free breakfast and luncheons . . . and free parking. . . .
> - *Increase the average GMAT score of your MBA class to above 650. . . .* You will need to decrease the number of students in the MBA program . . . and never admit students who have low GMAT scores, even if they otherwise show strong potential. . . .
> - *Increase services to recruiters,* including valet parking, free meals, gift baskets in hotel rooms, and a comfortable lounge area. . . .
> - *Eliminate not-for-profit programs and other MBA majors that produce graduates who are placed in low-salary positions.* . . .
> - *Entice everyone who inquires about [your] program, especially unqualified students, to apply. . . .* (U.S. News uses the number of admits divided by the number of applicants as a selectivity measure.) . . . .
> - *Increase the budget for the MBA program substantially; $50,000 per student is a good target . . .* you will need to reallocate funds . . . [for example, by decreasing] the size and/or the cost of delivery of your undergraduate [and doctoral] program[s] [and diverting] resources from the support of faculty research to the MBA programs . . . .
>
> (Quoted in Mintzberg, 2004: 78–79).

Professor Henry Mintzberg concludes this list by stating: "If you think that these suggestions seem tongue-in-cheek, think again. They are only a fraction of what many deans over the years have described to me as their "ranking strategy" (ibid: 79).

Consultant and author David Maister captures the essential difference between a measure and a judgment in a post on his blog:

> There is no quantitative system that cannot be "gamed." Some firms like to think that financial measures are "objective," but that's a delusion. They are not objective if people are making the numbers look good by hoarding work, failing to share and collaborate and thinking of their own metrics. What's objective about that? (http://davidmaister.com/print.php?n=blog&dl=12, accessed January 30, 2006).

Nevertheless, this one-metric mentality has recently been popularized by James Collins's 2001 best-selling book, *Good to Great: Why Some Companies Make the Leap . . . and Others Don't*:

> [W]e did notice one particularly provocative form of economic insight that every good-to-great company attained, the notion of a single "economic denominator." Think about it in terms of the following question: *If you could pick one and only one ratio—profit per x (or, in the social sector, cash flow per x)—to systematically increase over time, what x would have the greatest and most sustainable impact on your economic engine?* We learned that this single question leads to profound insight into the inner workings of an organization's economics.
>
> Walgreens switched its focus from profit per store to *profit per customer visit.* Convenient locations are expensive, but by increasing profit per customer visit, Walgreens was able to increase convenience (nine stores in a mile!) *and* simultaneously increase profitability across its entire system.
>
> [Or consider] Gillette: profit per customer. Key insight: Shift from profit per division to profit per customer reflected the economic power of repeatable purchases (e.g., razor cartridges) times high profit per purchase (e.g., Mach3, not disposable razors) (Collins, 2001: 104–106).

So what would be the one metric for a knowledge company? I don't know. Perhaps value created *per unit of intellectual capital,* but we do not yet have the tools and methodologies to measure this (though models do exist that try).

On the other hand, perhaps it is the wrong question. I side with management thinker Charles Handy. In a lecture to the Royal Society of Arts in London in 1996, he described "the fallacy of the single criterion":

> Trying to find one number that is the sum of everything is misguided. There is never any one number that will actually explain success in life and we are foolish ever to think that it might be there. Money certainly isn't it. Businesses know very well that profit is not the only measure. Sensible organizations now have about 18 different numbers they look at.

Nevertheless, the myth pervades our society that if you are profitable you are successful. Or if you're in the public sector, then efficiency is what matters. But efficiency is not quite the same as effectiveness. You can have a very efficient hospital if you don't take in very sick people or people who are not going to get better, like the old ones. So you push them outside. You're efficient but you're not terribly effective. Looking for the one number has corrupted our society (quoted in Boyle, 2001: 192).

Handy is right in one respect when it comes to the productivity of knowledge environments: the one criterion is not inputs based on cost or man-hours. That metric tells us nothing about how well a company is creating value. Maybe a more holistic, interdependent approach is needed, one whereby we strive to improve the means and enable the ends to take care of themselves. This is professor Johnson's argument.

Management by Means

We had been collecting tons of statistics because
they were interesting. But statistics will not construct
automobiles — so out they went.

—Henry Ford, *My Life and Work,* 1922

Imagine you're planning to construct a building, let us say a 50-story hotel. It has been estimated that most of the mistakes are made in such a project on the very first day. When just 1 percent of the project costs have been spent, up to 70 percent of its life-cycle costs have most likely been committed. It certainly pays to get the *process* right before you spend the first dollar, so you will end up with the results you want, at the right total cost.

This is what makes H. Thomas Johnson's book (coauthored with Anders Bröms), *Profit Beyond Measure,* such a seminal work, although not yet fully developed. And while I have severe misgivings about some of the environmental rants in the book, when he profiles Toyota and Scania—the latter now owned by Volvo—as two manufacturers that *do not* have a standard cost accounting system, he is on firm ground. It is hard to argue with results, and Toyota is one of the most respected companies in the world, having produced one of the highest-quality products at the lowest cost in the industry for years, dating back to 1926 when it started as a weaving machinery manufacturer. It has an unbroken record of profits, with zero layoffs, since 1960— a record unparalleled in the industry—and is a fierce innovator, ranking at the top in any measure of productivity you care to analyze.

As Glenn Uminger, a financial controller at Toyota Motor Manufacturing-Kentucky (TMM-K)—which Johnson studies in depth in this book—since 1988, says: "TMM-K has never had a standard cost system to track operating costs, and we probably never will." So how do they do it? How can a manufacturing company run without a standard cost accounting system? First, Toyota understands price drives costs, not the other way around. Here is how Johnson explains it:

> None of these comments is meant to imply that Toyota does not have accounting and production planning information systems. Of course it does. Toyota has a comprehensive array of information systems, accounting and otherwise, with which to *plan,* in advance of operations, and to *report* results of operations after the fact. But information from such systems is *not allowed to influence operational decisions* (Johnson and Bröms, 2000: 106).
>
> Toyota management discharges its responsibility for costs not by taking arbitrary steps to manipulate operations, but largely in the vehicle planning stage. During the design stage, long before the first penny has been committed to making a vehicle, Toyota has always placed enormous importance on setting and achieving cost targets. To do so, over the years Toyota has developed a famous technique for target costing. Simply stated, target cost is the maximum cost the company can afford to incur to produce and sell a vehicle and still earn a required profit at the price customers are expected to pay (ibid: 109).

Johnson goes on to explain his theory that Toyota operates under "management by means" rather than "management by results." It is an interesting viewpoint because it treats the organization as a living system, based on interdependent relationships, and those are nearly impossible to quantify. He notes Dr. Deming's observation that over 97 percent of the events that affect a company's results are not measurable, while less than 3 percent of what influences final results can be measured:

> Managers who adopt the new thinking offered here will accept as second nature the idea that what decides an organization's long-term profitability is the way it organizes its work, not how well its members achieve financial targets. This chapter compares the long-term records of Toyota and the American "Big Three" automakers to demonstrate the truth of this proposition. It posits Toyota's principles as an example of new management thinking called "management by means." Management by means is the antithesis of "managing by results," practices identified . . . with Toyota's American competitors. Those who manage by results focus on bottom-line targets and consider that achieving financial goals justifies inherently destructive practices. Those who manage by means consider

that a desirable end will emerge naturally as a consequence of nurturing the activities of all employees and suppliers in a humane manner. Managing by means requires a profound change in thinking that is a bold alternative to conventional management thinking and practice (ibid: 12).

Management accounting simply takes accounting revenue, cost, and profitability information, which is appropriate for measuring the overall financial results of a business, and inappropriately attempts to trace it to the particular activities and products of the business that gave rise to those results. Assigning such quantitative measures to parts of a mechanistic system makes sense. However, the parts of a natural living system cannot be so treated. Accounting measures are unable to penetrate the organic, multifaceted union between customer and company that ultimately is the source of a company's financial results. This union is the reason any company exists (ibid: 145).

Because cost and profit are not objects, but are properties that emerge from relationships, quantitative measures can only describe them, they cannot explain them. Quantitative measures, unlike art, music, or the stories and myths that humans fashion with words, cannot convey understanding of the multidimensional patterns that shape the relationships from which results, such as cost and profit, emerge in a living system (ibid: 188).

Henry Ford certainly agreed with this target-costing approach, because the most optimal time to plan total costs is *before* you build something, as he makes clear in his autobiography, *My Life and Work*:

Our policy is to reduce the price, extend the operations, and improve the article. You will notice that the reduction of price comes first. We have never considered any costs as fixed. Therefore we first reduce the price to the point where we believe more sales will result. Then we go ahead and try to make the prices. We do not bother about the costs. The new price forces the costs down. The more usual way is to take the costs and then determine the price; and although that method may be scientific in the narrow sense, it is not scientific in the broad sense, because what earthly use is it to know the cost if it tells you that you cannot manufacture at a price at which the article can be sold? (Ford, 1922: 146–47).

Notice Ford "never considered any costs as fixed." He understood, in the long run, all costs are avoidable, and by subjecting every cost to the test—does it add value to the customer?—he was able to lower the costs in the factory:

But more to the point is the fact that, although one may calculate what a cost is, and of course all of our costs are carefully calculated, no one knows what a cost ought to be. One of the ways of discovering what a cost ought to be is to name a price so low as to force everybody in the place to the highest point of efficiency. The low price makes everybody dig for profits. We make more discoveries concerning manufacturing and selling under this forced method than by any method of leisurely investigation (ibid).

Ford also understood the division of labor between a cost accountant and an effective factory foreman:

The rate of production and the cost of production are distinct elements. The rating of a department is gained by dividing the number of parts produced by the number of hands working. The foreman need not be a cost accountant—he is no better a foreman for being one. His charges are the machines and the human beings in his department. When they are working at their best he has performed his service. The rate of his production is his guide. There is no reason for him to scatter his energies over collateral subjects (ibid: 98–99).

Consider this example of paying attention to processes that add value for the customer, from Masao Inoue, chief engineer, Product Planning Division, Toyota Motor Corporation, discussing the new hybrid car, the Prius:

With the Prius we talk about quietness. Now noise can be measured by figures, but there is also a quietness that you feel with your body. For instance, with regard to the acceleration, the Prius is very different from other cars. You can time the speed of acceleration with a stopwatch, but the actual speed and the body's perception of it are very different. Of course, we do measure these things, and we get some target figures. But just because we get the target figure we are after, it doesn't mean it's okay. Figures are figures. We need to be able to feel the quietness or feel good about the acceleration as we actually experience it in the car. I think these things are very important (quoted in Roberts, 2005: 118).

The feel of a car often comes down to the small things, like the feel when you actually touch the material, leather, or wood. This is a new kind of thinking, thinking of how things feel to the consumer. To make my decisions, I must always ride in the car. There are many things that you cannot find from data that you discover when you ride in a car. There is nothing, no machine, that can replace the human body. It is the best sensor. For example, when you turn the steering wheel, sometimes you can just feel a sound. So faint you can't really measure it, but the feel of it is there. Also, things like the glove box, the console box, or the cup holder. When you open and close them they create their own sounds. And there are often faint sounds that can really irritate the person who is driving a car. The aim is to create a stillness that you can't actually measure by figures in the normal sense, and this is done by feeling and touch (ibid: 125).

As opposed to the cost accounting—or activity-based costing—concept of "cost drivers," managing by means uses "cost purposes." Cost drivers assume certain activities drive costs, irrespective of their relationship to revenue. Cost purposes, by contrast, are driven by those items that create value, hence are "blessed by revenue"; therefore, cutting costs to increase profitability is the equivalent of cutting purposes, reducing value and, hence, profits. Johnson concludes:

> Today's business leaders use cost accounting to control and assess the work that leads to results. You can use accounting to describe a business's external condition, but it offers little insight into the particular inner relationships that determine those results. It is unable to penetrate the organic union between customers and company that ultimately is the source of a company's financial results (Johnson and Bröms, 2000: 142, 145).

Johnson's argument particularly makes sense when you consider that in an industrial-age enterprise, value is largely created through transactions, and accounting systems are very proficient in recording these. Conversely, in an intellectual-capital enterprise, value is created by intangible investments in human, social, and structural capital, and precedes, sometimes by years, any transactions. This is certainly true with Amazon, Google, AOL, or pharmaceutical R&D. Accounting is far less proficient in understanding how these costs create value; hence it tends to treat them as period expenses, subject to cuts if times get tough. It illustrates well the dichotomy of cutting activities that drive cost at the expense of those that drive purpose.

The Austrian philosopher Ludwig Josef Johan Wittgenstein (1889–1951) wrote, "That which you do not know, you should shut up about." This is good advice for cost accountants, who are often wrong but never in doubt when it comes to determining the correlation between costs and creating value. Conventional training in cost accounting offers little help here, since it is not grounded in theory. Being able to audit the drunk's bar bill offers little help in changing his underlying behavior.

In a paper entitled "Reflections of a Recovering Management Accountant," which was presented at the Society for Organizational Learning prior to the publication of *Profit Beyond Measure,* Johnson included an open conversation where he was asked:

> *Peter Senge*: Tom, I don't think you said Toyota doesn't measure anything. You did say something about how they don't use the measures.
>
> *Johnson*: Yes, it's the way they don't use them that I find interesting, not the fact that they do not measure. Toyota measures, they just don't drive actions with quantitative targets.

Bill O'Brien: They don't use it to motivate action.

Johnson: Right, they don't use measures to drive decisions about how work should be done and what work should be done and so forth. Of course, they have an excellent accounting system. They invented what we call "target costing." But that's a descriptive measurement concept, really. It's an ex-ante tool, employed before the work is even started. But once the work begins, cost targets play no role in influencing operational decisions. The things that guide the work come from a different level of abstraction than quantitative measures come from. Guiding the work are things that aren't measurable. Over time, they develop systems and patterns of behavior that are deeply ingrained in people. These are deep disciplines they have in order to know "how is the work flowing?" Do we have a capability to detect normal from abnormal? These are the types of things they focus on, that everybody comes to know (Johnson, 1998: 11).

Andrew Carnegie's favorite saying was, "Watch the costs and the profits will take care of themselves." Kaplan would say, "Measure the result and the means will take care of themselves." Johnson is saying, "Nurture the means; the results will take care of themselves." And I argued in *Pricing on Purpose,* "Watch your value and the profits will take care of themselves." The truth, most likely, lies somewhere in between, which is why I have borrowed ideas from all of these thinkers. Though, I suspect even Peter Drucker might have agreed more with Johnson's approach:

I do not believe that one can manage a business by reports. I am a figures man, and a quantifier, and one of those people to whom figures talk. I also know that reports are abstractions, and that they can only tell us what we have determined to ask. They are high-level abstractions. That is all right if we have the understanding, the meaning, and the perception. One must spend a great deal of time outside, where the results are. Inside a business one only has costs. One looks at markets, at customers, at society, and at knowledge, all of which are outside the business, to see what is really happening. That reports will never tell you (quoted in Flaherty, 1999: 86).

LET THE DEBATE CONTINUE

No one business book will be able to settle this debate conclusively, and I will leave it up to the reader to think for him- or herself which method— or combination thereof—you believe is best for your organization. Perhaps a good way to think about this dichotomy is if you know exactly the behavior needed for a worker to perform his or her job, then input and productivity measures will probably work. If you don't know what a worker needs to do—as is the case with most knowledge work—then leave the worker alone to figure out the means and measure the results.

Theories only progress through dissension, so I look forward to the feud between managing by results versus means continuing. Central bankers have long understood what they term Goodhart's law: Any target that is set quickly loses its meaning as it comes to be manipulated. There has been a debate raging ever since the creation of central banking systems over whether monetary authorities should pay attention to interest rates or changes in the money supply. One finds compelling arguments on each side. But this may be a false choice. The Good Lord gave us two eyes, and one can be used to monitor results while the other watches the process.

To the extent companies continue to track lagging indicators, even with the Balanced Scorecard approach, this is little more than modern-day pantometry. To the extent they posit leading indicators that can actually be falsified, they will make progress in determining the real value drivers for customers. The experience with the Balanced Scorecard so far has been mixed, with some companies abandoning them. This, of course, does not falsify the basic premise—the companies in question could just have bad strategies—but it is a sign that companies need to pay closer attention to the processes that drive the financial results.

It is for this reason I find Johnson's argument more compelling, and more conducive to a knowledge environment. Of the two eyes, the one focused on financial results will always be more myopic, as this book has attempted to prove so far. In the knowledge economy, we are just going to have to become more comfortable with judgment and intuition over measurement and counting.

In any event, no matter which method you rely on, there is another characteristic that is essential to the definition of knowledge workers, and it is important since it goes against the conventional wisdom of how we have thought about this growing segment of the working population.

14

HUMAN CAPITAL, NOT CATTLE

In a few hundred years, when the history of our time is written from a long-term perspective, it is likely that the most important event those historians will see is not technology, not the Internet, not e-commerce. It is an unprecedented change in the human condition. For the first time—literally— substantial and rapidly growing numbers of people have choices. For the first time, they will have to manage themselves.

And society is totally unprepared for it.

—Peter Drucker, "Managing Knowledge Means Managing Oneself," 2000

The term *human capital* was first used by Nobel Prize–winning economist Theodore W. Schultz in a 1961 article in *American Economic Review.* His basic thesis was that investments in human capital should be accounted for in the same manner as investments in plant and machinery.

The obvious challenge is that investments in tangible, physical assets can be counted and comprehended ("kicked and ticked," in auditor parlance), but those in people cannot. Human capital is like the dark matter of the cosmos: we know it's out there but we can't measure it. Once again, Peter Drucker was at the forefront of thought when he coined both the terms *knowledge society* and *knowledge worker,* in 1961, and later expanded on this new phenomenon in his 1968 book, *The Age of Discontinuity.* He posited it was the G.I. Bill of Rights, passed in 1944—which made available higher education to some 2,332,000 veterans and was certainly the largest single investment in human capital up to that time—that caused the shift to a knowledge society.

Knowledge workers are not like workers from the Industrial Revolution who were dependent upon the employing organization to provide the means of production (factories and machines). Today, knowledge workers themselves *own* the firm's means of production—in their heads. This is a seismic shift in our economy, the ramifications of which we are still trying to comprehend. You can have an epiphany standing in the shower that is a multimillion dollar idea. How do we measure the output? Certainly not based on the cost of the inputs, or the amount of time spent showering, even including drying off.

KNOWLEDGE WORKERS ARE VOLUNTEERS

In an ironic twist on Karl Marx's idea of the proletarian revolution, in today's capitalist society, labor trumps capital as the chief source of all wealth. Your team members don't just contribute work, but also knowledge to the firm—they are *knowledge workers* in the purest sense. As knowledge workers age, their incomes rise, and this is consistent with the theory of human capital postulated by Schultz, Gary Becker, and other economists since.

In a factory, the worker serves the system; in a knowledge environment, the system should serve the worker. Knowledge work can only be designed *by* the knowledge worker, not *for* them. Unlike work on an assembly line, knowledge work is not defined by *quantity* but by *quality*. It is also not defined by its costs, but by its results, as we examined in Chapter 12.

Thinking in terms of human capital, investors lends dignity and respect to the value of each person. The word "human" comes from the Latin *Hominem,* for man, and the word "capital" from the Latin *caput,* meaning head. In other words, all capital ultimately springs from the mind. In a strict sense, a company's knowledge is created only by individuals—albeit some are outside of the firm's employ—and thus no knowledge can be created without people.

Moreover, the average knowledge worker today will outlive his or her employer, with an average productive work life of approximately 50 years, compared to the average organizational life of 30. This translates into the average knowledge worker having many more jobs—and even careers—than those of their predecessors a century ago. This has tilted the balance of power to the knowledge worker, as Drucker pointed out:

> In the knowledge society, the most probable assumption for organizations—and certainly the assumption on which they have to conduct their affairs—is that they need knowledge workers far more than knowledge workers need them (quoted in Boyle, 2001: 114).

Yet companies do not seem to understand the worth of their people. They treat them as if they were assets—or equally offensive, resources—rather than as investors of human capital who own their own—hence the firm's—means of production. And like most investors, they will go where they can earn a fair *economic* return—measured in wages, fringe benefits, and other pecuniary rewards—as well as where they are well treated and respected, the *psychological* return.

Labeling your people as assets is demeaning. Stalin used to say the same thing—and acted on it. People deserve more respect than a phone system or computer. Peter Drucker's 1946 book, *The Concept of the Corporation,* was a plea for General Motors to treat workers as a resource and not a cost, saying the most valuable thing about the workers was not their hands but their minds.

But labeling employees as resources—from the Latin *resurgere,* "to rise again"—is even worse, as if people were oil or timber to be harvested when you run out. Peruse a corporate annual report or talk to executives from anywhere in the world, and inevitably you will hear "people are our greatest asset" [or "resource"]. Even Michael Eisner, former chairman and CEO of Disney, has been recorded as saying "our inventory goes home at night." There's a new twist: people are now inventory to be turned over. Why do we insist on perpetuating this belief that people are resources to be mined rather than human capital to be developed?

There is a Chinese proverb that teaches the beginning of wisdom is to call things by their right names. Your people are not assets, resources, or inventory, but human capital investors seeking a decent return on their investment. In fact, your people are actually *volunteers,* since whether or not they return to work on any given day is completely based on their own volition. Consider for a moment how people decide which volunteer organizations to contribute some of their talent. It's usually based on a desire to contribute to something larger than themselves. They work hard—some would say harder than at their jobs—for these organizations because they are dedicated to the cause and they have the passion, the desire, and the dream to make a difference in the lives of others. All for zero pay. Why?

This is not just an economic decision, it is a psychological and emotional decision. With all this evidence of human behavior, many firms still treat their people as if they will slack off if they're not held accountable for every hour of every day. Is this any way to inspire people to be their best? Is this any way to instill a spirit of service and dedication to serving customer goals and aspirations? Or is this nothing but antiquated thinking about the nature of man being lazy and slothful unless forced to work?

So many leaders actually seem frightened at the thought of removing command-and-control hierarchies, as if they would be relinquishing total control over their team. Worse, they believe the suggestion is the equivalent of giving the team members total freedom, and will create anarchy in the organization. But I am not suggesting freedom for people "to do their own thing"; that is not freedom, it is *license*. The flip side of freedom is responsibility. By using the KPIs outlined in Chapter 12, you *are* holding people accountable for the *results* they achieve, hardly a prescription for anarchy and chaos. When leaders feel they need to tightly control a knowledge worker, they have made a hiring mistake.

It has been observed that most firm leaders could not lead a trail of ants to a picnic lunch. That may or may not be true—there is enough evidence to support either conclusion. But there is no doubting the fact that the antiquated measurement system of Taylorism is hindering the effectiveness of knowledge workers and eroding customer service. Since this is not even an effective method for measuring the *results* of knowledge workers, why do so many companies insist on clinging to these antiquated measurements for dear life, despite all of the evidence of superior alternatives?

There is no better way to demoralize knowledge workers than to have them perform duties that interfere with the tasks they are qualified to do. In all probability, the best way to increase the effectiveness of most knowledge workers is by *removing* various tasks that distract them from their core specializations. We do not want surgeons piercing ears or nurses spending half of their time completing paperwork (a common complaint). Most knowledge workers could easily stop doing approximately one-fourth of their tasks with no demonstrable loss of value.

FAR FEWER KNOWLEDGE WORKERS THAN WE THINK

My colleagues and I at VeraSage Institute spend the majority of our time working with, by any common definition, knowledge workers, at accounting, law, and technology firms; advertising agencies; consultancies; engineering, architecture, and software programming firms; and so forth. We educate them on the difference between manual (and service) workers, and knowledge workers. In a way, it is a compliment to be told you are part of a new wave of wealth creation in the economy by being labeled a knowledge worker. People take pride and immediate ownership in the term; you can even see a demonstrable increase in their self-esteem. It just feels good to be called a knowledge worker.

But I can always count on at least one of my colleagues to cause some cognitive dissonance, and Dan Morris has not let me down. He thinks I'm wrong about most professional firms being filled with knowledge workers; he believes the majority of them are more akin to factory workers in the days of Taylor. Now I know this is a heretical view, but Dan has assembled a very powerful argument to support his assertion. He does not deny professionals have the *potential* to be knowledge workers. His argument is they are not largely because of the incentives and structures of the firms in which they operate, which function more like sweatshops of yore.

This is a powerful argument, and it made me pause to reexamine my core assumptions about automatically asserting that just because people are credentialed professionals, or work with their heads more than their hands, they are automatically knowledge workers. There is no doubt they can contribute a certain amount of creativity and innovation to the jobs they perform and the customers they serve. But being a knowledge worker also requires that the leaders of your organization recognize and treat you like one. This is where Dan's more constricted definition of a knowledge worker is compelling.

Stephen Covey writes about exactly this in his latest book, *The 8th Habit: From Effectiveness to Greatness*: ". . . It's the leadership beliefs and style of the manager, not the nature of the job or economic era, that defines whether a person is a knowledge worker or not. If he is not perceived as a knowledge worker, that is, if a janitor is not seen as the local expert on janitorial work, then he is a manual worker and not a knowledge worker" (Covey, 2004: 265–66). I do not agree with this definition in its entirety. The major determinant of knowledge workers is that they *own the means of production,* and they apply knowledge to knowledge to create value. Covey's requirement of the leadership beliefs and style of management may be *necessary* conditions, but they are not *sufficient,* in and of themselves, to define knowledge work.

The same might be said regarding the knowledge worker's environment. The process of ethnography involves using multiple cameras to observe how workers interact in their environments in order to optimize spatial conditions. This has a certain ring of feng shui to it—that is, not at all scientific—but if it helps knowledge workers to be more comfortable in their environments, then it could be worthwhile.

Some companies have a "clean desk" requirement, thinking it helps to improve productivity if things are neat and orderly. This may be true for clerical work, whose mission is to help the company run smoothly. But knowledge workers use information to change themselves. The paper piles and Post-it Notes strung all over your office are physical representations of what is going on inside of your head. If anyone interferes with your desk, they interfere with your thinking, not a wise intrusion just to obtain 1 percent greater efficiency.

I remain skeptical of ethnography and other environmental factors because, once again, true knowledge work transcends time and space. J.K. Rowling wrote part of the first *Harry Potter* novel in an Edinburgh coffee

Exhibit 14.1   Paul O'Byrne, knowledge worker extraordinaire: Here are my dual monitors,[2] where's my productivity?

Photo by Paul O'Byrne

shop. In the old days, one took their coffee to the office. With Starbucks and knowledge workers, we now take our office to the coffee.

Having said all that regarding leadership beliefs and environmental factors, when you consider the metrics used by most professional service firms to measure their team members, they all come from the Industrial Revolution's command-and-control hierarchies (realization and utilization rates, billable hour quotas, etc). Yet, as discussed in Chapter 12, these productivity metrics are woefully inadequate at measuring a knowledge worker's effectiveness.

Dan further supports his argument by stating that leaders of knowledge workers:

- Don't impose billable hour quotas.
- Understand knowledge workers are paid for ideas, not hours, like union employees.

- Allow at least 15 percent of team member time for innovation and creating better ways to add value to customers. (This certainly destroys productivity under the old metrics.)

- Understand that *judgments* and *discernment* are far more important than *measurements* in assessing performance.

- Are focused on outputs, results, and value, not inputs, efforts, activities, and costs.

- Don't require timesheets that account for every 10 minutes of their day.

- Trust their workers to do the right thing for the firm and its customers.

- Recognize that individuals have value, not jobs.

- Allow their workers to monetize the value of their output, through stock options or other incentives that share the wealth created by minds, not machines.

- Select workers who are passionate and self-motivated and don't need constant supervision.

If these criteria describe your firm, congratulations, you are a true knowledge organization. Perhaps nothing illustrates the value knowledge workers can add to a business better than the announced purchase of Pixar by Disney, on January 24, 2006, for $7.4 billion in Disney stock. Disney will have to respect Pixar's culture and continue to let it make quality movies at its own pace, in its own way. Otherwise, if Pixar's creative talent leaves, "Disney just purchased the most expensive computers ever sold," according to Lawrence Haverty, a fund manager at Gabelli Asset Management. It remains to be seen whether Disney can learn from Steve Jobs' philosophy: "You cannot mandate productivity, you must provide the tools to let people become their best."

Knowledge workers need to be able to monetize at least part of the wealth they create, which is based on contribution, not seniority or stultifying union-type job classifications. Real knowledge work transcends time and space and can take place anywhere, while innovation is actually more likely to come from those team members with far less seniority, since most breakthrough innovations happen before the age of 45. If stock options, or other incentive plans, are not offered in order to attract and retain talent, firms will not be able to tap into the enormous wealth-creating potential of their knowledge workers.

There is an old military saying that instructs the soldier is entitled to competent command. Unfortunately, most professional firms that we at

VeraSage have come into contact with around the world do not fit Dan's criteria, which is why he makes such a strong case that they function more like manual laborers—or service workers—than actual knowledge workers. After all, if one set out to find knowledge workers, you would naturally select professional service firms as the most likely place to find them.

I cannot count the number of times we have been asked by intelligent firm owners, "How would I know what my team members were doing if they didn't complete a timesheet?" This is not a question demonstrating fear over lack of control, this is the *illusion* of control. Someone can look great on a timesheet, but do substandard work, have a poor customer service attitude, or disrupt colleagues, or a myriad other poor characteristics that cannot be captured on a timesheet. But because the leaders in these firms do not trust the judgment of the people they hire, they feel they need to micromanage them. This is counterproductive. Knowledge workers cannot be told *how* to do their job, since many understand the job at hand better than their bosses. They cannot be held accountable for results if their methods are micromanaged.

I do not intend to dwell on the debate over the word "manager" versus "leader," but in the specific context of knowledge work it is interesting to ponder where "manager" comes from:

> *Manager* is derived from the old Italian and French words *maneggio* and *manège,* meaning the training, handling and riding of a horse. It is strange to think that the whole spirit of *management* is derived from the image of getting on the back of a beast, digging your knees in, and heading it in a certain direction. The word *manager* conjures images of domination, command, and ultimate control, and the taming of a potentially wild energy. It also implies a basic unwillingness on the part of the people to be managed, a force to be corralled and reined in. All appropriate things if you wish to ride a horse, but most people don't respond very passionately or very creatively to being ridden, and the words *giddy up there* only go so far in creating the kind of responsive participation we now look for. Sometime over the next fifty years or so, the word manager will disappear from our understanding of leadership, and thankfully so. Another word will emerge, more alive with possibility, more helpful, hopefully not decided upon by a committee, which will describe the new role of leadership now emerging. An image of leadership which embraces the attentive, open-minded, conversationally based, people-minded person who has not given up on her intellect and can still act and act quickly when needed (Whyte, 2001: 240–41).

It is obvious executives who are responsible for knowledge workers are going to have to become much more comfortable with intuition, judgment, and discernment over measurements. You simply cannot manage people by numbers. Professor Henry Mintzberg—who defends the word manager over leader—tells the story of one student who asked him: "How can you select for intuition when you can't even measure it?" (Mintzberg, 1989: 83). This is a sad commentary on the state of current MBA education. We seem to be turning out greyhounds in counting but ignoramuses in dealing with human beings.

Emotions are essential to good decisions, since "most people reason dramatically, not quantitatively," as Oliver Wendell Holmes once wrote. This is why people are inspired more by stories than spreadsheets and pie charts full of statistics. Martin Luther King didn't proclaim, "I have quarterly objectives," but spoke of having a dream.

So many leaders are worried that if they get rid of objective measures they will introduce subjective bias into the decision-making process. So what? That's exactly what needs to happen. We simply cannot measure the most important things in life. To get rid of bias we would have to give up judgment, which is too high a price to pay. Neurologist Antonio Damasio has studied brain-damaged patients, demonstrating that without emotion it is impossible to make decisions. Why would we want to give up our human emotions? For as accurate or scientific as you can make any measurement, judgment and intuition are more important, as they are in chess, according to world chess champion, since 1984, Garry Kasparov (who won, and lost, to IBM's Deep Blue supercomputer):

> People who see chess as a scientific pursuit played by some kind of human supercomputer may be surprised, but it takes more than logic to be a world-class chess player. Intuition is the defining quality of a great chess player. That's because chess is a mathematically infinite game. The total number of possible different moves in a single game of chess is more than the number of seconds that have elapsed since the big bang created the universe. Many people don't recognize that. They look at the chessboard and they see 64 squares and 32 pieces and they think that the game is limited. It's not, and even at the highest levels it is impossible to calculate very far out. I can think maybe 15 moves in advance, and that's about as far as any human has gone. Inevitably you reach a point when you've got to navigate by using your imagination and feelings rather than your intellect or logic. At that moment, you are playing with your gut.
>
> Often, your gut will serve you better than your brains. I've been working now on a five-volume book called *My Great Predecessors,* which reviews the development of the game of chess by looking closely at the playing histories of the great players of the past 200 years. When analyzing their games together with a computer, I found something very

interesting. It was often at the very toughest moments of their chess battles—when they had to rely on pure intuition—that these great players came up with their best, most innovative moves. Ironically, when the games were finished and the players had the luxury of replaying them for publication, they typically made many more mistakes than they did when actually competing. To me the implication is clear: What made these players great was not their analytic prowess but their intuition under pressure (Kasparov, 2005).

The fact that we cannot describe within any degree of certainty the characteristics of a knowledge worker vivifies how much work is left to be done in this field. Nobel Prize-winning economists have yet to figure it out, so one more business book is not going to be the final word on an issue nearly 50 years old. Clarence Darrow expressed it well when he said, "To think is to differ," and this is certainly the case with knowledge workers.

What we do know is that people are not machines you can program for greater productivity, or bags of cement you can move around to achieve your ends. It didn't work for the Nazis or the Soviet Union and it certainly will not work in a knowledge organization. Until leaders begin to treat their workers as outlined in Dan's argument, we are a long way from reaping the true rewards of an intellectual capital economy.

KNOWLEDGE WORKERS OF THE WORLD UNITE!

Jim Casey, founder of UPS in 1907, said in 1947: "A man's worth to an organization can be measured by the amount of supervision he requires." Isn't it time companies recognize they are dealing with knowledge workers, not Taylor's factory workers? Knowledge work is not subject to the same rhythms and cadences as an assembly line; it is an iterative process of the mind, and the traditional time-and-motion studies are out of place in the modern knowledge firm.

It is time for the firms of the future to remove the sword of Damocles—objective measurements hanging over the head of their workers—and unleash them from a theory no longer applicable to the modern intellectual capital economy. It requires leadership and vision. It requires knowing you are doing the right thing, not just doing things right. It requires focusing the company on the external results it creates for customers and simultaneously building the type of organization people are proud to be a part of and invest their intellectual capital in. It requires an attitude of experimentation, not simply

**Exhibit 14.2   Karl Marx's Tomb,
Highgate Cemetery,
London.**

Photo by Paul O'Byrne

doing things because that is the way it has always been done. It requires less measurement and more trust.

To paraphrase from the last lines in Karl Marx's *The Communist Manifesto:* "Knowledge workers of all countries, unite! You have nothing to lose but your timesheets."

15

THE MORAL HAZARDS
OF MEASUREMENTS

*I could never convince the financiers that Disneyland was
feasible, because dreams offer too little collateral.*

—Walt Disney

Exact measurements of the wrong things can drive out good judgments of
the right things. There are a plethora of things man can measure, but without being guided by theory, a lot of those measures would be meaningless.
Max De Pree's story humorously illustrates this point:

> Buckminster Fuller, the philosopher, inventor, and designer . . . was
> touring a new building that an excellent architect, Norman Foster, had
> just completed in the English countryside. Norman had carefully pre-
> pared for the visit and had asked his staff to anticipate every question
> Bucky could possibly pose. As Norman and Bucky approached the
> building, which looked as if it could have been a huge extrusion landed
> in the meadow by a giant helicopter, Norman reviewed in his mind
> all the answers, all the angles.
>
> Bucky went along silently as they moved through the impressive build-
> ing. At last he turned and pierced Norman with his steady, twinkling gaze
> and asked simply, "How much does it weigh? (De Pree, 1989: 127–28).

The illusion of certainty in our measurements creates—to borrow an
important concept from the insurance industry—a *moral hazard*. Simply
defined, people have an incentive to take more risks or act carelessly when
they are insured. Fire insurance causes arson; unemployment insurance allows
people to not be as diligent in finding a job; life insurance causes suicide,
or worse, murder; auto insurance can cause reckless driving; federal disaster
insurance enables people to build on floodplains, or other places suscep-
tible to natural disasters, since they do not suffer the costs of their choices.

If people are insured, they may just act carelessly and cause the very thing they are insured against.

Our current cult of calculation, perpetuated by the infamous McKinsey maxim—what you can measure you can manage—creates the same type of risk, offering today's business executives the illusion of control and mastery of knowledge. It allows them to substitute statistics for thinking. It gives them a false sense of security where there should exist more doubt; for as Francis Bacon so aptly wrote, in 1605, in *The Advancement of Learning*: "If a man will begin with certainties, he shall end in doubts, but if he will be content to begin with doubts, he shall end in certainties." Many times, numbers prove nothing, such as in start-ups, whose financial statements may look horrible but which may some day rise like the phoenix from the ashes and decimate the status quo infrastructure in a particular industry. The process of serendipity, trial and error, creativity, and discovery is just too impossible to measure, so the tendency is to ignore it as noise, subjective judgment, opinions, or just plain luck. The dog always barks at what it doesn't understand.

When the disposable-diaper product Pampers was launched, it was intended for the travelers' market; it was never even thought of as a product people would use at home. Apple Computer's business plan did not mention the education market at all, yet it turned out to be one of its major triumphs. When George Parker played a prototype version of the game Monopoly, invented by Charles Darrow, he found it too complicated and technical, issuing a rejection letter in 1934 that cited "52 fundamental errors." Subsequently, he had to swallow his words—and his pride—and bought back the game, which in two years had sold 2 million units. Parker displayed his scornful rejection letter to Darrow in public as a lesson in humility.

All enterprise is an act of faith, a world where the leap is more important than the look. This is why no government has been able to guarantee jobs—because it can't control what customer preferences will be in the future. Dogs do not lie because they cannot talk; and the market—just an aggregation of billions of individuals—also doesn't lie because the ultimate arbiter of value is the customer. And value is subjective; like beauty, it is in the eye of the beholder. Which is why enterprise is fraught with risk. Customers are fickle, one day fondling their iPods and the next the latest gadget to replace it, with no nostalgia for past attachments. They are heartless and merciless with respect to their preferences, which quickly can disrupt the economics of entire industries or any one company. People will not stand still long enough to be counted or measured, which is why the "perennial gale of creative destruction" that the great Austrian economist Joseph Schumpeter so eloquently wrote about is such a conundrum. Economists, politicians, sociologists, and others can measure and count the *destruction,* but not the *creativity.* The destruction is highly visible—the closed factory, the laid-off workers, the ghost towns—while the *creativity,* today just a flicker in the mind of the entrepreneur, or a start-up struggling to make payroll, is next to impossible to capture in numbers. In government, this process of trial and error is called *waste;* in the private sector, it is called *risk,* and is the impetus behind progress, dynamism, and economic growth.

If we want to peer into the unknown future, our measures need to be linked to a theory, otherwise we are simply predicting the past—since history is the only dimension for which numbers can provide precision. Without theory, we are simply modern-day pantometrists, counting because we can. With theory, we can measure what matters, not simply download our mental models by using statistics as a way to confirm our existing assumptions about the status quo. With theory, we can also avoid the *moral hazards of measurements* so prevalent in today's society.

THE SEVEN MORAL HAZARDS OF MEASUREMENTS

> *As long as measurements are abused as a*
> *tool of control, measuring will remain the weakest*
> *area in a manager's performance.*
>
> —Peter Drucker

The United State's attempt to measure the Soviet Bloc economies during the Cold War was the largest social-science project ever undertaken, yet the various governmental agencies involved consistently overstated the size and growth rate of the communist countries. The eponymous textbook written by economist Paul Samuelson declared, as late as 1986, that the Soviet Union economy was the fastest-growing among industrial nations between 1928 and 1983, growing at 4.9 percent per annum. The conservative economist Henry C. Wallich was so bamboozled by these statistics that he wrote *The Cost of Freedom,* in 1960, arguing political and economic freedom comes at the price of lower economic growth.

The 1989 edition of the *Statistical Abstract of the United States,* a Bureau of the Census publication, draws on data provided by a wide range of government agencies, including the Central Intelligence Agency. One of the published estimates was the size of the economies of the Federal Republic of

Germany and the German Democratic Republic, or West Germany and East Germany, as they were then known. Per capita output in 1985 in both countries was shown to be *equal,* with the gross domestic product of East Germany slightly higher. In the *Handbook of Economic Statistics 1989,* per capita output in 1988 in East Germany—one year before the Berlin Wall was pushed over—was placed at roughly seven-eighths of the West German level.

But as any Berlin taxi driver crossing through Checkpoint Charlie after the fall of the Wall could have told you, the economy of East Germany was manifestly inferior to that of West Germany, yet somehow—due to the moral hazard of measurement—those in the know got it precisely wrong rather than approximately right. Taking into account the following seven moral hazards of measures may assist executives in avoiding these types of errors.

Moral Hazard 1: We Can Count Consumers, But Not Individuals

Singer Joan Baez used to say it was easier for her to have a relationship with 100,000 people than with one person. Stalin's famous remark that "one death is a tragedy, whereas a million is a statistic" illustrates the danger of lumping individuals into aggregate, amorphous lumps as if they did not have a soul.

Stanley Marcus, the son of one of the founders of Neiman-Marcus, led the store through the difficult Great Depression, and one point he was especially fond of making was there was no such thing as a market, only customers:

> I am unaware of any store, or any business school, for that matter, that conducts a course or a series of lectures on "The Care and Treatment of Customers." I am referring to "customers" and not "consumers," for never in my retail experience have I ever seen a "consumer" enter a store. I've seen lots of "customers," for that's what they call themselves (Marcus, 1979: 211).

At first glance, this is a contestable statement. Business executives, and certainly economists, pore over macroeconomic data of markets, trends, demographics, lumping individuals into amorphous segments. No doubt this type of analysis is useful, but Marcus's point is compelling once given serious consideration. In 2003, General Motors sold 8.59 million vehicles, yet each was sold *one at a time.* The micro level, where the customer interacts with the seller, is inherently a flesh-and-blood transaction. As economist Herbert Stein always used to say, "There is nobody here but us people." In the final analysis, markets and consumers are statistical abstractions, whereas *customers* are human beings who want to be treated specially and individually.

Jean Parker, the training director of Neiman-Marcus during Marcus's leadership, gave this advice to every new class of salespeople:

> Every one of you has been a customer. You have different reasons for buying in different stores from different salespeople. Now you're going to be on the other side of the counter. Don't think for one minute that all the people with whom you will be dealing shop for the same reason. Every customer is an individual (ibid: 153).

We have all dealt with organizations that treat everyone the same, such as the United States Postal Service or the local cable company. It is not very inspiring service, which is why KPIs must ultimately evolve to the individual customer level. One cannot achieve this standard if you view people as statistics, whose individual costs and benefits can be summed up in what Jeremy Bentham labeled "felicific calculus." Because benefits and costs are inherently personal and subjective, aggregation misses the individual. We can measure the objective temperature in a room at 70 degrees, but any one person may feel either warm or cold, and the differences cannot be used to cancel each other out. We simply cannot mathematically manipulate people.

Moral Hazard 2: You Change What You Measure

Scientists call it Heisenberg's Uncertainty Principle, which applies to all measures: that the observer in a scientific experiment affects the result. Central bankers call it Goodhart's law: Any target that is set quickly loses its meaning as it comes to be manipulated. People will always find ways to make their numerical targets, even if it leads them to ineffective or, sometimes, unethical behavior.

A further hazard lies in the fact that in order to count something it must stand still, which is why the first statisticians were called "statists." But people don't stand still; they are constantly moving, changing, growing. Human action is what the Austrian economist Ludwig Von Mises (1881–1973) called *purposeful behavior.* It is free will put into action. In contrast, a billiard ball moves because it is hit by another; it can't decide for itself. In physics, 3 laws explain 99 percent of the data; in finance and economics, 99 laws explain 3 percent of the data. This explains why economists have physics envy. But, admittedly, they have a tougher job since even a physicist cannot explain why a car goes to Wal-Mart rather than Kmart.

Moral Hazard 3: Measures Crowd Out Intuition and Insight

Once a measure becomes entrenched as part of the conventional wisdom, it is usually impenetrable to logic, intuition, critical thinking, or better ways to do something. Poverty statistics are a perfect example, as everyone accepts them as a precise measure of those citizens living below what we consider an acceptable standard of living. But how was this measure developed? Where did it come from? This story has been little told.

The poverty rate measures the *income* of the poor, not their *consumption,* which is a false talisman of someone's standard of living. It is not what you *earn,* it is what you are capable of *spending*; thus consumption should be measured, which would take into account nonreported earnings, noncash subsidies, and other services provided. It is also a national statistic, and does not take into account regional differences in the cost of living. Further complicating the error, during the Johnson administration's war on poverty, it was decided the "poverty rate" would be set at an arbitrary three times the cost of the U.S. Department of Agriculture's economy food plan, as explained by Nicholas Eberstadt in his book *The Tyranny of Numbers*:

> Looking back on her work in the early 1960s, Mollie Orshansky, the Social Security Administration researcher credited with constructing the poverty rate, noted that the initial decision to set the official poverty line at three times the cost of the U.S. Department of Agriculture's economy food plan "endowed an arbitrary judgement with a quasi-scientific rationale it otherwise did not have" (Eberstadt, 1995: 272).

On August 30, 2005, the Census Bureau released its poverty estimate for the year 2004, concluding 12.7 percent of the population lived in deprivation, comparing it to the 11.2 percent for 1974, 30 years earlier. In a September 9, 2005, *New York Times* editorial, "Broken Yardstick," Eberstadt, a researcher with the American Enterprise Institute, summed up the problem with the current poverty statistic:

> So why did that poverty rate report end up mostly buried deep inside daily papers?
>
> Maybe because many news editors, like policymakers in Washington, know the dirty little secret about the poverty rate: it just isn't any good. Truth be told, the official poverty rate not only fails to calculate trends in impoverishment with any precision, it even gets the direction wrong.
>
> In the Labor Department's latest Consumer Expenditure Survey (2003), the average reported income for the bottom fifth of households was $8,201, while reported outlays came to $18,492—well over twice that amount. Over the past generation, that discrepancy widened significantly: back in the early 1970's, the poorest fifth's reported spending exceeded income by 40 percent.
>
> For now, however, we should recognize that America has already achieved far more success in the war against want than our sorry poverty

rate can admit—and that we need much better guidance systems for the anti-poverty battles still ahead than this one, arguably the single worst measure in our government's statistical arsenal (Eberstadt, 2005).

Using a consumption-based, rather than an income-based, poverty measure, Eberstadt has concluded elsewhere that the rate drops from approximately 13 percent to between 2 and 3 percent. Quite a difference, and illustrative of how far off even old measurements can be and how firmly entrenched they remain despite being precisely wrong. But even if we were competent enough to measure with exactitude the poverty rate, it would shed no light on how to lift people out of it. This is why Adam Smith studied *wealth,* since it is the best-known antidote to poverty. There is an old Scottish proverb particularly relevant to this discussion: "You don't make sheep any fatter by weighing them."

This is where H. Thomas Johnson's approach, documented in Chapter 13, of "managing by means" versus "managing by results," is triumphant. We need deeper understanding and new processes to lower the poverty rate, not better measures. In a business context, another example illustrates how accurate statistics do not help drive better performance until they are combined with a theory.

If you have ever been bribed off an oversold airplane—with a free flight voucher, upgrade, or airline money equivalent—you have economist Julian Simon (1932–1998) to thank. Until 1978, and before the airlines were deregulated, travelers were bumped off overbooked planes rather capriciously (the airlines preferred to bump old people and military personnel on the theory they would be least likely to complain) and this caused enormous amounts of customer complaints and ill will. Sometimes an entire flight would be cancelled and rebooked at proper capacity, causing even greater outrage. Worse yet, the problem fed upon itself, because passengers began to expect being bumped and so would book several flights under various names to ensure a seat on at least one. This caused the airlines to increase bookings even more to ensure decent load factors, which of course were measured very precisely. A flight attendant friend who worked for United Air Lines told Simon of this problem:

> The next day when shaving it occurred to me that there must be a better way; indeed, an auction market could solve the problem by finding those people who least mind waiting for the next flight. The practical details fell into place before the shave was complete.
>
> In 1966 and 1967 I wrote to all the airlines suggesting the scheme. The responses ranged from polite brushoffs, to denials that they overbooked, to assertions that the scheme could not work, to derision.

> . . . I was unable to persuade any airline (or the Civil Aeronautics Board) to conduct an experiment for even one day on a single airline at a single airport at a single boarding gate—an experiment that I believed would be sufficient, even with the inevitable breakdowns in any new activity.

> (Simon, 2002: 289–94).

Had the airlines changed the process and tested Simon's idea sooner, the airlines and its customers both would have been better off. Simon did not analyze countless numbers and statistics, but used his intuition, grounded by the economist's theory of human behavior being rational, to solve a quite vexing problem. Daniel Boorstin, librarian of Congress, wrote: "The greatest obstacle to discovery is not ignorance—it is the illusion of knowledge." To the extent our illusions of knowledge come from precise measurements that drive out critical thinking, we should constantly "hang our assumptions in front of us" to challenge our prevailing theories and look for better ways to do things.

Moral Hazard 4: Measures Are Unreliable

We have already seen how a country's per capita gross domestic product increases when a sheep is born but decreases when a child is; or how divorce actually increases the GDP since almost two of every commodity must now be purchased rather than just one. Whether it is the statistics that attempt to measure a country's GDP, poverty, or the financial statistics we use to assess the health of a business, we take for granted that just because they have the imprimatur of a governmental agency or an auditing firm they are beyond reproach. This is demonstrably false.

Oskar Morgenstern (1902–1977), former Princeton University economist wrote a fascinating—and devastating—little book challenging the value of many types of economic statistics. *On the Accuracy of Economic Observations* makes many specific salient points with respect to what he terms the "specious accuracy" of many statistics. He defined two types of specious accuracy: irrelevance and functional, the latter having a very small margin of error but nevertheless useless.

He tells the story of one of the chief European figures (he is not identified) of government describing how they will get more money out of the Marshall Plan:

> We shall produce any statistic that we think will help us to get as much money out of the United States as we possibly can. Statistics which we

do not have, but which we need to justify our demands, we will simply fabricate" (Morgenstern, 1963: 21).

The point is that many of these bogus statistics ended up in the official historical records, compounding the errors of statistical and econometric analysis ever since. Morgenstern even made the point of how so many of the processes in a modern economy are interrelated and defy measurement, by sharing this amusing story:

> During World War II, the production of optical instruments was temporarily greatly hampered by a shortage of babies' diapers. The reason was that diapers were an excellent polishing material for lenses. Surely in an input-output table a zero transaction between these two industries would have seemed more plausible than a purchase of diapers by optical companies! (ibid: 133).

He further pointed out that when two unreliable statistics are multiplied or divided, the error is magnified even further. This type of error is not limited to economics or business, as the sciences suffer the same flaw. The difference is, in economics or business, the textbooks are silent with respect to what should be done about it. He offered this prescription to counter specious accuracy:

> . . . [S]top important government agencies, such as the President's Council of Economic Advisors, the various government departments, the Federal Reserve Board and other agencies, public and private, from presenting to the public economic statistics as if these were free from fault. Statements concerning month-to-month changes in the growth rate of the nation are nothing but absurd and even year-to-year comparisons are not much better. . . . It is for the economists to reject and criticize such statements which are devoid of all scientific value, but it is even more important for them not to participate in their fabrication. . . . [E]conomic decisions, by business and government alike, are made largely in the dark (ibid: 304–5).

In an ironic twist of history, economist John Maynard Keynes said much the same thing in his magnum opus, *General Theory*:

> Too large a portion of recent "mathematical" economics are mere concoctions, as imprecise as the initial assumptions they rest on, which allow the author to lose sight of the complexities and interdependencies of the real world in a maze of pretensions and unhelpful symbols (quoted in Gilder, 1993: 286).

Of course, this statement is ironic since Keynes' *General Theory* launched the Keynesian revolution in economics, ushering in the belief that the federal government could fine-tune the economy using his theory of manipulating fiscal policy—government spending and taxation—in order to stimulate or depress macroeconomic activity as needed. The decade of the 1970s, with its perpetual stagflation falsified Keynes' theory, which led economic historian Thomas Sowell to quip, "Keynesian economists thought they could fine-tune the economy, but they'd be lucky to get the right channel."

Even a company's balance sheet and income statement are subject to a margin of error that is never adequately disclosed to shareholders and other interested parties. Nor do financial statements make a distinction between revenue (or profits) increasing or decreasing due to inflation or deflation, or better pricing, for example. The former is external to the firm's control, while the latter can be influenced by executive decisions internally; yet the financials are mute as to the difference. We have already seen how generally accepted accounting principles (GAAP) do a pathetic job of measuring—or even acknowledging—intellectual capital. Why would we want to put so much faith in these numbers? Picasso once said, "Art is a lie that tells the truth." It seems in some instances, measurements are truths that tell lies.

Nevertheless, if you are acclimated to driving with a faulty speedometer, perhaps the best thing you can do is go on using it. You may drive worse if you have the speedometer repaired. It in no way absolves you of admitting to the error, and if you are not rooted in theory there is no way to determine cause and effect.

Another example of the unreliability of measures is illustrated by the consulting firm Bain & Company's home page on its Web site (www.bain.com/bainweb/home.asp), where it proudly proclaims: "Our clients outperform the market 4 to 1," shown over a graph from 1980 to 2004 depicting the S&P 500 Index and Bain clients (accessed February 24, 2006). This is the equivalent of the rooster taking credit for the sunrise because he crows every morning. One expects this type of unscientific hyperbole from politicians, not management consultants. I would be willing to bet that Bain's clients perform better than the S&P 500, thus have more money to spend on consultants.

Executives need to be far more sensitive to the errors in the data they use to make decisions. Many measures do not have the authority of the Oracle of Delphi, and we need to show more humility and less arrogance with respect to what we do not know. Einstein was very cognizant of this fact, stating, "One single new fact could suffice to invalidate the whole theory of relativity."

Moral Hazard 5: The More We Measure the Less We Can Compare

Engage in this gedanken: You (or a loved one) need(s) heart surgery. You talk to nurses, friends, and other people you trust and respect, and two surgeons are consistently recommended to you. You go online to do some research on these two practitioners and discover their mortality rates (i.e., the risk of dying from surgery): surgeon A = 65 percent; surgeon B = 25 percent. Which surgeon would you choose?

I have conducted this gedanken in seminars attended by various educated professionals—who certainly have taken a statistic class or two—and, astonishingly, the overwhelming majority select surgeon B. When I ask why, they say because of the lower probability of death. Perhaps they think they need to choose between the two without gathering other information. But that is not how I set up the thought experiment: I left it open as to whether they could ask further questions. Almost none do.

But wouldn't you want to know what type of patients the two doctors serve? What if surgeon A takes a disproportionate share of hard cases and thus has a higher failure rate? He or she just may be the better surgeon. The point is, we simply do not know without gathering more information, both quantitative and qualitative, and making further judgments based on our own risk profile. Seeing the two numbers side by side seems, though, to give people a false sense of precision and, in this case, could lead to a deadly decision.

In a more prosaic setting, this happens when businesses engage in ruthless imitation of other companies, cloaked in the names of benchmarking and best practices. Rather than investing in R&D and experimenting with innovation, a lot of companies are spending precious executive resources trying to figure out where they are relative to the competition, by studying financial indicators and other forms of competitive intelligence.

While no doubt useful for some applications, benchmarking is not a way to build a strategic advantage. It is as if entire industries are gazing at each other's navels, rather than looking for ways to change the rules of the game. Poring over lagging indicators such as financial ratios—debt-to-equity, net income percentages, labor as a percentage of revenue, and so on—rarely spurs innovation and dynamism within an industry. Ultimately, you cannot know how to do something you've never done before; otherwise, there could be no innovation. Comparative information has a place, but it must be tempered with a theory of what is being observed if we are to gain an understanding of the underlying causes.

The major problem with benchmarking studies and best practice reports is you are studying the *results* of a process, not the process itself. It tends to confuse cause and effect, and we are back to man trying to fly by strapping on wings and jumping off of cliffs rather than studying the theory of aerodynamics. The Roman poet Ovid wrote: "The cause is hidden; the effect is visible to all."

Financial averages can be devastatingly misleading without understanding the underlying causes of the results you are observing; after all, you can prove statistically that everyone in the world has, on average, one testicle. The average is where the worst of the best meets the best of the worst. Further, there is a *selection bias* in the data being analyzed; rarely is it a truly random sample or a statistically significant sample size.

Avoid benchmarking your competitors—why benchmark mediocrity? Truly effective benchmarking usually takes place outside of one's industry, such as when Henry Ford was inspired to create the assembly line from a visit to a slaughterhouse where he observed the overhead trolley system. What was standard in one industry became a revolution in another—old ideas in new places. Mark Twain probably said it best:

> The best swordsman in the world doesn't need to fear the second-best swordsman in the world. No, the person for him to be afraid of is some ignorant antagonist who has never had a sword in his hand before; he doesn't do the thing he ought to do, and so the expert isn't prepared for him; he does the thing he ought not to do, and often it catches the expert out and ends him on the spot (quoted in Peters, 2003: 298).

We simply cannot compare two doctors, two universities, or two hospitals based on measures alone. It takes subjective evaluation, discernment, and intuition. History is the science of human biography, not measures, and we can no more compare two countries' cultures by examining their GDPs than we can compare two people by the size of their bank accounts.

Moral Hazard 6: The More Intellectual the Capital, the Less You Can Measure It

Economists have a joke they use to describe the factory of the future. It will have just one man and one dog. The man's job is to feed the dog. The dog's job is to keep the man from touching the equipment (quoted in Gersemann, 2004: 53). This may be funny, but it is not likely in an economy dominated, more and more, by intellectual capital—mind over matter. Ideas only come from sentient beings, not inanimate objects or pets. Since 75 percent of any country's wealth-creating capacity resides in its human capital, how could it be otherwise?

To complicate matters, a lot of that knowledge is tacit, which is hard to capture in spreadsheets and pie charts. We may be able to count the physical assets of a Google or a Microsoft, but traditional accounting pays no attention to its human capital, what has been labeled the "invisible balance sheet." Traditional book value accounting—assets minus liabilities equals equity—can only explain about one-fourth of the value of the market capitalization on the nation's stock markets. Accountants call the difference between market value and book value goodwill; but that is just a label for their ignorance. In an intellectual capital economy, debits don't equal credits, because value is subjective and flows from free minds, not tangible commodities.

The old canard—usually expounded by noncreative types—that good ideas are everywhere and it is really execution that matters, would be relatively easy to overcome if only it were true. But it is not true; for if it were, we would have better movies (not remakes of *Bewitched* and *The Dukes of Hazzard*), books, and other products; more memorable experiences; and longer-lasting transformations from the companies we patronize. Both ideas and execution are important. There is no effective way to implement a bad idea, and history provides many lessons, from Napoleon invading Russia to countries attempting to implement socialism. Were these bad ideas or simply cases of poor execution?

In his last book, *The Effective Executive in Action,* Peter Drucker explained the decision-making process:

> A decision is a judgment. It is a choice between alternatives. It is rarely a choice between right and wrong. It is at best a choice between "almost right" and "probably wrong" . . .
>
> But executives who make effective decisions know that one does not start with facts. One starts with opinions. These are, of course, nothing but untested hypotheses and, as such, worthless unless tested against reality (Drucker and Marciariello, 2006: 184)
>
> Then no one can fail to see that we start out with untested hypotheses —in decision-making as in science the only starting point. We know what to do with hypotheses—one does not argue them; one tests them (ibid: 186).

Data, reason, and calculation can only produce conclusions; they do not inspire action. Good numbers are not the result of managing numbers. As David Boyle wrote in *The Sum of Our Discontent:* "Decisions by numbers are a bit like painting by numbers. They don't make for great art" (Boyle, 2001: 41). General Electric's successful Work-Out initiative was the program Jack Welch began, in 1988, with Jim Baughman, who headed General Electric's Crotonville management development center. The concept behind Work-Out was "to convey the idea of getting the nonsense 'worked-out' of General Electric, . . . to make themselves lean and agile . . ." (quoted in Mintzberg, 2004: 225). Even though Jack Welch was a proponent of Six-Sigma and other rational measurement systems, he refused to measure the impact of Work-Out: "[I]t'd die if they started to measure and track the results it was producing. Instead, he'd know in his gut when it was working and when it was not" (quoted in ibid: 345).

Knowledge work is difficult to measure; of course that does not mean we should not measure what we can. It does mean we should not let measures drive out common sense, emotions, and judgment—our gut, as Jack Welch says. Oliver Wendell Holmes once wrote: "We are mere operatives, empirics, and egotists, until we learn to think in letters instead of figures."

Moral Hazard 7: Measures Are Lagging

Imagine driving your car with your dashboard gauges informing you of last month's speed, fuel level, temperature, oil pressure, RPMs, and the rest. This is precisely the status of accounting information: it is like walking into the future backward. It is a lagging indicator—or at best coincident, assuming real-time accounting takes place. This type of information can only tell us where we have been, never where we are going. Auditors come in after the battle and bayonet the wounded; they are historians with lousy memories. As Reid Buckley (William F. Buckley's younger brother) so wittily points out in his book, *Sex, Power, and Pericles*:

> Straight logical progression is the ticket when what one wants is the facts and nothing but the facts, ma'am. This is what you desire when you ask your accountant or CFO for the financial status of your company. Is it operating at a profit or a loss? Period. The good Lord spare anyone a CPA who draws up an emotional or mystical/religious presentation of his company's financial shape, or who indulges in poetic flights of the imagination when what a person needs to know is how much boodle he must part with to meet his payroll taxes.
>
> The accountant may validly analyze the numbers advanced in support of vision, but his report on past performance is never predictive, and his opinion on the validity of the vision itself is worthless. Past performance may be a commentary on current performance, never a harbinger of future performance. It can't be.
>
> Yesterday's profit and loss statement is as useful in foretelling what tomorrow may bring as poking about in the entrails of birds or dipping tea leaves (Buckley, 1996: 38–9).

The present accounting model is over 500 years old and is in bad shape. The traditional GAAP financial statements are based on a liquidation value of a business, essentially historical cost assets less liabilities—a heroic attempt to assign static value to a dynamic concern. The balance sheet dates from 1868, the income statement from before World War II. The P&L statement was set up to account for the most important cost in an industrial society: cost of goods sold. But in a knowledge economy, cost of goods sold—or cost of revenue—is less meaningful, with Microsoft averaging 14 percent of sales, Coca-Cola roughly 30 percent, and Revlon 34 percent. Even though intellectual capital is the main driver of wealth, you will look in vain to find it in the traditional GAAP statements—the balance sheet, income statement, and statement of cash flows. Increasingly, these statements are being referred to as the "three blind mice."

Enron and the other spate of accounting scandals from the early 2000s were not so much about fraud, malfeasance, misfeasance, or other crimes, but rather the increasing *irrelevance* of the traditional accounting reporting model. Enron's legerdemain is not what caused it to fail. Its financial deception allowed it to remain in business for longer than an otherwise similar firm engaged in accurate financial disclosures, but this is a question of *timing* alone and not *causality*. The financial statements were simply lagging indicators of bad business decisions. Had Enron been reporting leading indicators, perhaps the market could have responded sooner. As Talleyrand said about the shooting of the Duke d'Enghien, *"C'est pire qu'un crime, c'est une erreur* (It's worse than a crime, it's a mistake).

Compounding the mistake was the passage of the Sarbanes-Oxley Act of 2002, which will not restore relevance to GAAP. All it does is pile burdensome and costly regulations onto a decrepit reporting model no longer relevant to an intellectual capital economy. This is the equivalent of Baron Munchausen's struggle to extract himself from a swamp by pulling on his own hair.

The accounting profession is a mature profession, and its last true innovation was the financial statement compilation and review standards, effective in 1978. This is a 28-year innovation curve, and counting. Additional governmental regulations will only slow this innovation down further. (Heavily regulated industries are rarely innovative. If the computer industry were as heavily regulated as auditors and accountants, we would have Vacuum Tube Valley, probably located in West Virginia.)

The French economics journalist Frédéric Bastiat (1801–1850) wrote in 1850: "There is only one difference between a bad economist and a good one: the bad economist confines himself to the visible effect; the good economist takes into account both the effect that can be seen and those effects that must be foreseen." Nearly everyone accepts the need for regulation. The debate, therefore, is not over whether we ought to have regulation but about the best way of doing so.

That being said, we need to keep in mind that in a free market economy, innovation and dynamism are the lifeblood of wealth creation. Profits come from risk. Yet from Prometheus—who democratized fire by taking it from the gods and making it accessible to mankind—onward, societies have feared the innovation and the innovator. The recent securities fraud shareholder suits and the SEC fines imply the current demand is for risk-free investment opportunities. The current whine seems to be, "They didn't tell me I could lose money!" We seem to want the trial without the error (or to privatize the gains and socialize the risks). This is simply an impossible objective.

What we heard prior to the passage Sarbanes-Oxley was the "market failure" argument. Yet what is never considered is that when regulations are put into effect they often substitute market failure with government failure. Enron, WorldCom, and the rest have gone bankrupt, and its leaders are facing criminal and other sanctions. Arthur Andersen is gone. The SEC, on the other hand, will get a bigger budget and even more regulatory authority. The very agency that was established to "protect the investor" failed cataclysmically, and emerges with greater power and authority. This is subsidizing failure, and we can be sure of one thing: it will happen again.

In the spirit of Bastiat's unseen effects, one result of the Sarbanes-Oxley Act will be to increase the *moral hazard* of investing, because investors will now believe that new regulations have created a safer environment than is in fact the case. The result is they will take more risks than they otherwise would (similar to what happened when deposit insurance increases passed by Congress led to the moral hazard of savings and loans engaging in riskier business dealings in the 1980s, knowing that if they failed they would be bailed out by the government).

The Danish philosopher Søren Kierkegaard wrote: "Life is lived forward but understood backward." Certainly measures help us reflect on past events and aid us in improving our theories. But they can never take the place of dreams, imagination, passion, and the spirit of enterprise where entrepreneurs toil and struggle to create our future. George Gilder articulates it well:

> Knowledge emerges not from chaos, or fixity, but from conditions of uncertainty. Under capitalism power flows to precisely the people who are willing to stake their money not on gambles or sure things but on testable hypotheses, thus generating knowledge and wealth for society. Entrepreneurs are trustworthy because they accept a moral code of testability and falsifiability rather than one based on sentiment, sanctimony, good intentions, good press, good luck, good looks or guarantees (Gilder, 2002).

No measure is capable of capturing the richness of free minds operating in free markets dreaming of better ways to improve our future, and it is folly to believe otherwise. It may even lead us into moral hazards, or a world where we are so preoccupied about measuring past performance we do not take the time to dream about the future.

16

THE DREAMERS VERSUS THE PANTOMETRISTS

*I would rather live in a world where my life is
surrounded by mystery than live in a world so small
that my mind could comprehend it.*

—Harry Emerson Fosdick

Friedrich A. Hayek, the 1974 Nobel Prize winner in economics, believed the human mind could not see its own advance; the future is unpredictable, and we simply cannot know now what still remains to be known. Measuring and counting only give us a look at the past, and for all their presumed precision— as we examined throughout this book—numbers are full of imprecision and may lead to wrong conclusions. Theory does better, as it allows us to peer into the future, perhaps even to some small extent control it, but we can never predict it with absolute certainty.

I, for one, would not want to live in a world where the future is knowable and rational, a population comprised of automatons calculating with logical precision exactly what needs to be done to optimize current performance, whether in a business or society. Dreams always die when they come true. "Without measureless and perpetual uncertainty," Winston Churchill said, "the drama of human life would be destroyed."

Imagine if the founders of the United States, after signing the Declaration of Independence, had sent it to King George in Britain, who then replied as perhaps a modern-day MBA, corporate strategist, or accountant would reply today:

Dear Mr. Jefferson:

We have read your Declaration of Independence with great interest. Certainly it represents a considerable undertaking, and many of your statements do merit serious consideration. Unfortunately, the Declaration as a whole fails to meet recently adopted specifications for proposals to the Crown. So we must return the document to you for further refinement.

The questions that follow might assist you in your process of revision.

In your opening paragraph you use the phrase "the Laws of Nature" and "Nature's God." What are these laws? In what way are they the criteria on which you base your central arguments? Please document, with citations, from recent literature.

In the same paragraph you refer to "Opinions of Mankind." Whose polling data are you using? Without specific evidence it seems to us the "Opinions of Mankind" are a matter of—opinion.

You hold certain Truths to be "self-evident." Could you please elaborate? If they are as evident as you claim, they should not be difficult for you to locate the appropriate supporting statistics.

"Life, Liberty, and the Pursuit of Happiness" seem to be the goals of your proposal. These are not *measurable goals*. If you were to say that among these are the ability to sustain an average life expectancy in 6 of the 13 Colonies of at least 55 years; and to enable newspapers in the Colonies to print news without further interference; and to raise the average income of the Colonists by 10 percent in the next 10 years —these would be *measurable* goals. Please clarify.

You state, ". . . that whenever any Form of Government becomes destructive of these Ends, it is the Right of the People to alter or to abolish it, and to institute new Government . . ." Have you weighed this assertion against all other alternatives? What are the trade-off considerations?

Your description of the existing situation is quite extensive. Such a long list of grievances should precede the statement of goals, not follow it. Your problem statement needs improvement.

Your strategy for achieving your goals is not developed at all. You state the Colonies ". . . ought to be, Free and Independent States" and that you are ". . . absolved from all Allegiance to the British Crown . . ." Who or what must change to achieve this objective, and in what way must they change? What specific steps would you take to overcome the resistance? How long will it take? We have found that a little foresight in these areas might help to prevent careless errors later on.

How cost-effective are your strategies? Who among the list of signatories would be responsible for implementing your strategy? Who conceived it? Who provided the theoretical research? Who will constitute the advisory committee? Please submit an organisation chart and vitae of the principal investigators.

What impact will your problem have? Your failure to include any assessment of this inspires little confidence in the long-range prospects of your undertaking.

We hope that these comments prove useful in revising your Declaration of Independence.

We welcome submission of your revised proposal. Our due date for unsolicited proposals is 31 July, 1776. Ten copies with original signatures will be required.

Sincerely,
Management Analyst to the British Crown[1]

Dr. Ebeling, president of the Foundation for Economic Education, who conceived this thought experiment, concluded with a profound question: "I'd like to ask if the founding fathers had to have worked within such a framework, would we be independent today?"

The framers did not ask the following six questions that are always reasonable when individuals or organizations are confronted with a significant change, but when asked too soon and taken too literally may actually postpone the future and keep us encased in our present way of thinking. Peter Block describes these six questions in his insightful book, *The Answer to How Is Yes: Acting on What Matters*: How do you do it? How long will it take? How much does it cost? How do you get those [other] people to change? How do we measure it? How have other people done it successfully? (Block, 2003: 15–23).

How would Thomas Jefferson have answered these six questions?

- I don't know.
- I don't know.
- Possibly your life.
- I don't know.
- I don't think you can measure Life, Liberty, and the Pursuit of Happiness.
- No country has ever done it successfully the way we are proposing. Sign here.

Block suggests two better starting questions: "What [type of future] do we want to create together?" and "What is the price [we are] willing to pay to achieve it?"(ibid: 29, 32). It is simply impossible to know how to do something until you attempt it. In a free market system, it is the leap, not

---

[1] I am eternally indebted to Dr. Richard Ebeling, president of the Foundation for Economic Education, for the idea and the wording of this thought experiment, transcribed from an introduction Dr. Ebeling gave at an "Evenings at FEE event." See Ebeling, 2004, in the Bibliography for more information.

the look, that generates the indispensable understanding and the necessary knowledge to generate wealth. There is no security, only a world of risk and uncertainty, where one must humbly serve the needs of others—supply before you can demand—against a constant tidal wave of rising customer expectations, with no guarantee of sustainable success. A world where companies "built to last" only exist in book titles, not in the "perennial gale of creative destruction" necessary to propel the economy forward.

BUILT TO LAST VERSUS DYNAMISM

For my part, I would not like to live in a world where companies last forever. This is the ideology of communism and socialism, not a vibrant and dynamic free market economy. If a business is no longer creating wealth for its customers I want the market—meaning sovereign customers—to ruthlessly drive it out of business for wasting society's resources. Steve Jobs expressed his spirit for Apple this way:

> To me, Apple exists in the spirit of the people who work there and the philosophies and purpose by which they go about their business. If Apple becomes a place where computers are a commodity item, where the romance is gone, and where people forget that computers are the most incredible invention that man has ever invented, I'll feel I have lost Apple. (quoted in Young, 2005: 128).

I, too, would want Apple to vanish, replaced by some other entity with a fanatical commitment and passion for computers (and I have been a devoted Apple owner since 1984!). I do not want to inhabit a world built from the economist's perfect competition model, where businesses do nothing but crank out commodities on a "level playing field," with no ability to effect prices, output, or customer preferences. How dreadfully boring. No innovation, no dynamism, no growth.

I look forward to the *destruction* capitalism produces as much as I do the *dynamism*. Silicon Valley may be a fount of creativity, but only because it rests atop a mass cemetery of bankrupted hypotheses—many more new ventures fail than succeed—falsified by the sovereignty of the customer. Henry Ford wrote, "The man who is too set to change is dead already. The funeral is a mere detail" (Ford, 1922: 239). The same applies to companies, which is why capitalism creates prosperity—it has a built-in falsification process whereby companies, like scientific experiments, can be proven wrong and removed from wasting society's oxygen. It is not survival of the fittest; it is survival of only those firms that continue to add more value to society than they consume.

Traditional organizations rest on a command-and-control hierarchy supported through meticulous measurement and the quest for ruthless efficiency. Knowledge organizations are going to have to operate within a framework of personal autonomy and responsibility, built on a foundation of virtue. We need to start measuring what matters, enlightened by adaptable theories, which measure success the same way customers do. Positing and testing leading indicators—the equivalent of the coal miners' canaries—is a better talisman for aligning the processes in a knowledge organization to produce wealth, the main objective of any business.

We should not be subservient to facts and figures, allowing them to crowd out the qualities that comprise human dignity—intuition, imagination, judgment, passion, love, virtue, faith, hope, and charity. Civilization deserves no less. The most important things in life cannot be measured. The future belongs to the dreamer and the poet, not the pantometrist and rationalist.

BIBLIOGRAPHY

Albrecht, Karl. *The Only Thing That Matters: Bringing the Power of the Customer into the Center of Your Business.* New York: HarperBusiness, 1992.

————. *The Northbound Train: Finding the Purpose, Setting the Direction, Shaping the Destiny of Your Organization.* New York: American Management Association, 1994.

Albrecht, Karl and Ron Zemke. *Service America in the New Economy.* New York: McGraw-Hill, 2002.

Aquila, August J., and Allan D. Koltin. "How to Lose Clients without Really Trying." *Journal of Accountancy,* May 1992: 67–70.

Baker, Ronald J. *Professional's Guide to Value Pricing,* 6th ed. Chicago, IL: CCH Incorporated, 2005.

————. *The Firm of the Future: A Guide for Accountants, Lawyers, and Other Professional Services.* Hoboken, NJ: John Wiley & Sons, Inc., 2003.

————. *Pricing on Purpose: Creating and Capturing Value.* Hoboken, NJ: John Wiley & Sons, Inc., 2006.

Basch, Michael D. *Customer Culture: How FedEx and Other Great Companies Put the Customer First Every Day.* Upper Saddle River, NJ: Prentice Hall, 2002.

Beatty, Jack. *The World According to Peter Drucker.* New York: Free Press, 1998.

Becker, Gary S. *Human Capital: A Theoretical and Empirical Analysis, with Special Reference to Education,* 2nd ed., Midway Reprint. Chicago, Illinois: The University of Chicago Press, 1983.

Bernstein, Peter L. *Against the Gods: The Remarkable Story of Risk.* Hoboken, NJ: John Wiley & Sons, Inc., 2001.

Berra, Yogi, with Dave Kaplan. *When You Come to a Fork in the Road, Take It!: Inspiration and Wisdom from One of Baseball's Greatest Heroes.* New York: Hyperion, 2001.

Bethune, Gordon. *From Worst to First: Behind the Scenes of Continental's Remarkable Comeback.* New York: John Wiley & Sons, Inc., 1998.

Birla, Madan. *FedEx Delivers: How the World's Leading Shipping Company Keeps Innovating and Outperforming the Competition*. Hoboken, NJ: John Wiley & Sons, Inc., 2005.

Block, Peter. *The Answer to How Is Yes: Acting on What Matters*. San Francisco: Berrett-Koehler Publishers, Inc., 2003.

Boulton, Richard E. S., Barry D. Libert, and Steve M. Samek. *Cracking the Value Code: How Successful Businesses Are Creating Wealth in the New Economy*. New York: HarperBusiness, 2000.

Boyle, David. *The Sum of Our Discontent: Why Numbers Make Us Irrational*. New York: Texere, 2001.

Branden, Nathaniel. *Self-Esteem at Work: How Confident People Make Powerful Companies*. San Francisco: Jossey-Bass Publishers, 1998.

Buckley, Reid. *Sex, Power, and Pericles: Principals of Advanced Public Speaking*. Camden, SC: Peor Es Nada Press, 1996.

Caroselli, Henry M. *Cult of the Mouse: Can We Stop Corporate Greed from Killing Innovation in America?* Berkeley, CA: Ten Speed Press, 2004.

Cerf, Christopher, and Victor Navasky. *The Experts Speak: The Definitive Compendium of Authoritative Misinformation*. New York: Villard, 1998.

Christensen, Clayton M., and Michael E. Raynor. *The Innovator's Solution: Creating and Sustaining Successful Growth*. Boston: Harvard Business School Press, 2003.

Christensen, Clayton M., Scott D. Anthony, and Erik A. Roth. *Seeing What's Next: Using the Theories of Innovation to Predict Industry Change*. Boston: Harvard Business School Press, 2004.

Cialdini, Robert B. "Harnessing the Science of Persuasion," *Harvard Business Review*, October, 2001: 72–79.

Cohen, I. Bernard. *The Triumph of Numbers: How Counting Shaped Modern Life*. New York: W.W. Norton & Company, 2005.

Collins, James C., and Jerry I. Porras. *Built to Last: Successful Habits of Visionary Companies*. New York: HarperBusiness, 1997.

Collins, James C. *Good to Great: Why Some Companies Make the Leap . . . and Others Don't*. New York: HarperBusiness, 2001.

Covey, Stephen R. *The 8th Habit: From Effectiveness to Greatness*. New York: Free Press, 2004.

Davenport, Thomas H. *Thinking for a Living: How to Get Better Performance and Results from Knowledge Workers*. Boston: Harvard Business School Press, 2005.

Dawson, Ross. *Developing Knowledge-Based Client Relationships: The Future of Professional Services*. Boston, MA: Butterworth Heinemann, 2000.

De Pree, Max. *Leadership Is an Art.* New York: Dell Publishing, 1989.

Dickens, Charles. *Hard Times.* New York: Oxford University Press, 1998 (World's Classic Paperback Edition).

Dougherty, Peter J. *Who's Afraid of Adam Smith?: How the Market Got Its Soul!* Hoboken, NJ: John Wiley & Sons, Inc., 2002.

Drucker, Peter F. *Managing in a Time of Great Change.* New York: Truman Talley Books/Dutton, 1995.

———. *Management Challenges for the 21st Century.* New York: HarperCollins, 1999.

———. "Managing Knowledge Means Managing Oneself." *Leader to Leader,* 16, Spring 2000: 8–10.

———. *Managing in the Next Society.* New York: Truman Talley Books, 2002.

———. *Peter Drucker On the Profession of Management.* Boston, MA: Harvard Business School Publishing, 2003.

Drucker, Peter F., with Joseph A. Maciariello. *The Daily Drucker: 366 Days of Insights and Motivation for Getting the Right Things Done.* New York: Harper-Business, 2004.

———. *The Effective Executive in Action: A Journal for Getting the Right Things Done.* New York: Collins, 2006.

Ebeling, Richard M. Introduction to Dr. Richard Pipes, "Property and Freedom: The Inseparable Connection." Evenings at FEE, October 9, 2004. Available in audio format at: www.fee.org/events/detail.asp?id=6196&page=3&t=0.

Eberstadt, Nicholas. *The Tyranny of Numbers: Mismeasurement and Misrule.* Washington, DC: AEI Press, 1995.

———. "Broken Yardstick." *New York Times,* September 9, 2005. Accessed from www.nytimes.com/2005/09/09/opinion/09eberstadt.html?ex=1140930000 &en=21ddf481ab9d15f6&ei=5070, February 24, 2006.

Flaherty, John E. *Peter Drucker: Shaping the Managerial Mind.* San Francisco: Jossey-Bass Publishers, 1999.

Florida, Richard. *The Rise of the Creative Class: And How It's Transforming Work, Leisure, Community and Everyday Life.* New York: Basic Books, 2002.

———. *The Flight of the Creative Class: The New Global Competition for Talent.* New York: HarperCollins, 2005.

Ford, Henry, and Samuel Crowther. *My Life and Work.* Kessinger Publishing, 1922.

Friedman, David D. *Hidden Order: The Economics of Everyday Life.* New York: HarperBusiness, 1996.

Gersemann, Olaf. *Cowboy Capitalism: European Myths, American Reality.* Washington, DC: Cato Institute, 2004.

Gilder, George. *Wealth and Poverty.* New York: Basic Books, Inc., 1981.

————. *The Spirit of Enterprise.* New York: Simon and Schuster, 1984.

————. *Recapturing the Spirit of Enterprise: Updated for the 1990s.* San Francisco: ICS Press, 1992.

————. *Wealth and Poverty: A New Edition of the Classic.* San Francisco: ICS Press, 1993.

————. "The Gilder Friday Letter." *Gilder Technology Report,* Friday, December 13, 2002.

Gladwell, Malcolm. *The Tipping Point: How Little Things Can Make a Big Difference.* London: Abacus, 2000.

————. *Blink: The Power of Thinking without Thinking.* New York: Little, Brown and Company, 2005.

Gray, Scott. *The Mind of Bill James: How a Complete Outsider Changed Baseball.* New York: Doubleday, 2006.

Hamel, Gary. *Leading the Revolution.* Boston: Harvard Business School Press, 2000.

Hazlitt, Henry. *Economics in One Lesson.* New York: Crown Publishers, Inc., 1979.

Herman, Arthur. *How the Scots Invented the Modern World: The True Story of How Western Europe's Poorest Nation Created Our World and Everything in It.* New York: Three Rivers Press, 2001.

Hoopes, James. *False Prophets: The Gurus Who Created Modern Management and Why Their Ideas Are Bad for Business Today.* Cambridge, MA: Perseus Publishing, 2003.

Johnson, H. Thomas, and Robert S. Kaplan. *Relevance Lost: The Rise and Fall of Management Accounting.* Boston: Harvard Business School Press, 1991 [Original publication 1987].

Johnson, H. Thomas. "Reflections of a Recovering Management Accountant." Paper presented to the Society for Organizational Learning Initiative, First Research Forum, January 14–16, 1998. Accessed from www.solonline.org/repository/download/johnson.html?item_id=443237, September 24, 2005.

Johnson, H. Thomas, and Anders Bröms. *Profit Beyond Measure: Extraordinary Results through Attention to Work and People.* New York: Free Press, 2000.

Kaplan, Robert S., and David P. Norton. "The Balanced Scorecard: Measures That Drive Performance." *Harvard Business Review,* July–August, 2005:172–80.

Kasparov, Garry. "Strategic Intensity: A Conversation with World Chess Champion Garry." *Harvard Business Review,* April, 2005: 50.

Kay, John. *Foundations of Corporate Success: How Business Strategies Add Value.* New York: Oxford University Press, 1995.

Kehrer, Daniel. *Doing Business Boldly.* New York: Times Books, 1989.

Kihn, Martin. *House of Lies: How Management Consultants Steal Your Watch and Then Tell You the Time.* New York: Warner Business Books, 2005.

Krass, Peter, ed. *The Book of Entrepreneurs' Wisdom: Classic Writings by Legendary Entrepreneurs.* New York: John Wiley & Sons, Inc., 1999.

Landsburg, Steven E. *The Armchair Economist: Economics and Everyday Life.* New York: Free Press, 1993.

———. *Price Theory and Applications,* 5th ed. Cincinnati, OH: South-Western, 2002.

Lev, Baruch. *Intangibles: Management, Measurement, and Reporting.* Washington, DC: Brookings Institution Press, 2001.

Levine, Robert A. *A Geography of Time: The Temporal Misadventures of a Social Psychologist, or How Every Culture Keeps Time Just a Little Bit Differently.* New York: Basic Books, 1997.

Lewis, Michael. *Moneyball: The Art of Winning an Unfair Game.* New York: W.W. Norton & Company, 2003.

Low, Jonathan, and Pam Cohen Kalafut. *Invisible Advantage: How Intangibles Are Driving Business Performance.* Cambridge, MA: Perseus Publishing, 2002.

Maister, David, Charles H. Green, and Robert M. Galford. *The Trusted Advisor.* New York: Free Press, 2000.

Marcus, Stanley. *Quest for the Best.* New York: Viking Press, 1979.

———. *The Viewpoints of Stanley Marcus: A Ten-Year Perspective.* Denton, TX: University of North Texas Press, 1995.

———. *Minding the Store: A Memoir.* Denton, TX: University of North Texas Press, 1997 (facsimile edition of original publication, 1974).

———. *Stanley Marcus from A to Z: Viewpoints Volume II.* Denton, TX: University of North Texas Press, 2000.

McCloskey, Deirdre. *How to Be Human—Though an Economist.* Ann Arbor, MI: The University of Michigan Press, 2000.

McKenna, Patrick J., and David H. Maister. *First Among Equals: How to Manage a Group of Professionals.* New York: Free Press, 2002.

McNamara, Robert. *In Retrospect: The Tragedy and Lessons of Vietnam.* New York: Crown, 1995.

Medved, Michael. *Right Turns: Unconventional Lessons from a Controversial Life.* New York: Crown Forum, 2004.

Micklethwait, John, and Adrian Wooldridge. *The Witch Doctors: Making Sense of the Management Gurus.* New York: Times Books, 1996.

Miniter, Richard. *The Myth of Market Share: Why Market Share Is the Fool's Gold of Business.* New York: Crown Business, 2002.

Mintzberg, Henry. *Mintzberg On Management: Inside Our Strange World of Organizations.* New York: Free Press, 1989.

———. *Managers Not MBAs: A Hard Look at the Soft Practice of Managing and Management Development.* San Francisco: Berrett-Koehler Publishers, Inc., 2004.

Mokyr, Joel. *The Gifts of Athena: Historical Origins of the Knowledge Economy.* Princeton, NJ: Princeton University Press, 2002.

Morgenstern, Oskar. *On the Accuracy of Economic Observations,* 2nd ed. Princeton, NJ: Princeton University Press, 1963.

Morris, Edmund. *Dutch: A Memoir of Ronald Reagan.* New York: Random House, 1999.

Murray, Charles. *Human Accomplishment: The Pursuit of Excellence in the Arts and Sciences, 800 B.C. to 1950.* New York: HarperCollins Publishers Inc., 2003.

Myers, David G. *Intuition: Its Power and Perils.* New Haven, CT: Yale University Press, 2002.

Niven, Paul R. *Balanced Scorecard: Maximizing Performance and Maintaining Results.* Hoboken, NJ: John Wiley & Sons, Inc., 2002.

Nonaka, Ikujiro, and Hirotaka Takeuchi. *The Knowledge-Creating Company: How Japanese Companies Create the Dynamics of Innovation.* New York: Oxford University Press, 1995.

O'Kelly, Eugene. *Chasing Daylight: How My Forthcoming Death Transformed My Life.* New York: McGraw-Hill, 2006.

Paulos, John Allen. *I Think, Therefore I Laugh: The Flip Side of Philosophy.* New York: Columbia University Press, 2000.

Peters, Tom. *Re-Imagine!: Business Excellence in a Disruptive Age.* London: Dorling Kindersley Limited, 2003.

Reichheld, Frederick F., and Thomas Teal. *The Loyalty Effect: The Hidden Force Behind Growth, Profits, and Lasting Value.* Boston: Harvard Business School Press, 1996.

Reichheld, Frederick F. *Loyalty Rules! How Today's Leaders Build Lasting Relationships.* Boston: Harvard Business School Press, 2001.

Roberts, Kevin. *Lovermarks: The Future Beyond Brands.* New York: PowerHouse Books, 2005.

Shipler, David. "Robert McNamara and the Ghosts of Vietnam: Robert McNamara Meets the Enemy." *New York Times Magazine,* August 10, 1997.

Simon, Julian L. *A Life Against the Grain: The Autobiography of an Unconventional Economist.* New Brunswick, NJ: Transaction Publishers, 2002.

Skousen, Mark. *The Making of Modern Economics: The Lives and Ideas of the Great Thinkers.* Armonk, NY: M.E. Sharpe, 2001.

Sowell, Thomas. *Knowledge and Decisions.* New York: Basic Books, Inc., 1980.

———. *Basic Economics: A Citizen's Guide to the Economy.* New York: Basic Books, 2000.

———. *Basic Economics: A Citizen's Guide to the Economy,* Revised and Expanded Edition. New York: Basic Books, 2004.

Stewart, Thomas A. *Intellectual Capital: The New Wealth of Organizations.* New York: Currency, 1997.

———. *The Wealth of Knowledge: Intellectual Capital and the Twenty-First Century Organization.* New York: Currency, 2001.

Stigler, George J. *The Economist as Preacher and Other Essays.* Chicago: The University of Chicago Press, 1982.

Taylor, Frederick Winslow. *The Principles of Scientific Management.* New York: W.W. Norton & Company, 1967.

von Mises, Ludwig. *Human Action: A Treatise on Economics.* San Francisco: Fox & Wilkes, 1996.

Whyte, David. *Crossing the Unknown Sea: Work as a Pilgrimage of Identity.* New York: Riverhead Books, 2001.

Winston, William J., ed. *Marketing for CPAs, Accountants, and Tax Professionals.* New York: Haworth Press, 1995.

Young, Jeffrey S., and William L. Simon. *iCon: Steve Jobs, the Greatest Second Act in the History of Business.* Hoboken, NJ: John Wiley & Sons, Inc., 2005.

Yutang, Lin. *The Importance of Living.* New York: Quill, 1998 ed.

SUGGESTED READING

*Books constitute capital. A library book lasts as long as a
house, for hundreds of years. It is not, then, an article of mere
consumption but fairly of capital, and often in the case of
professional men, setting out in life, it is their only capital.*

—Thomas Jefferson: Letter to
James Madison, September, 1821

There is always a risk in recommending books to others, similar to arranging a blind date, which is perhaps why Fred Smith said in an interview with *USA Today,* "There are only about six business books worth reading. For enduring lessons, read history." Nevertheless, I will assume the risk and suggest several books I know will increase your intellectual capital.

All of the following books are included in the Bibliography, hence publisher and copyright date are omitted here.

Ronald J. Baker, *Professional's Guide to Value Pricing.* The author's first book, written specifically for accountants, lawyers, and other professional service firms. It challenges the pricing-by-the-hour paradigm (a form of cost-plus pricing) and offers alternatives for professionals to get out from under the artificial ceiling imposed—on themselves—by the billable hour, while offering alternatives to maintaining timesheets.

Ronald J. Baker and Paul Dunn, *The Firm of the Future: A Guide for Accountants, Lawyers, and Other Professional Services.* This book explores the old and new practice equations for leveraging intellectual capital in today's knowledge economy. Topics discussed include intellectual capital, customer selection, pricing, key performance indicators, leadership, and issues facing the professions.

Ronald J. Baker, *Burying the Billable Hour; Trashing the Timesheet;* and *You Are Your Customer List.* This series was published by the Association of Chartered Certified Accountants (ACCA), the world's largest, fastest-growing international professional accountancy organization, with nearly 300,000 members and students in 160 countries. You can download these books (in pdf format) for free from the ACCA Web site: www.accaglobal .com/?view=Search+results&freesearch=Burying+the+Billable+Hour.

Ronald J. Baker, *Pricing on Purpose: Creating and Capturing Value.* The first book in the Intellectual Capitalism Series, it discusses the old and new business equations, the labor versus subjective theories of value, cost-plus pricing's epitaph, price-led costing, what and how people buy, the value proposition, price discrimination, Baker's Law, ethics of pricing, antitrust law, the concept of a chief value officer, and an extensive bibliography and suggested reading list.

Gordon Bethune, *From Worst to First: Behind the Scenes of Continental's Remarkable Comeback.* An excellent narrative on how one of the worst airlines was transformed into one of the best, in a few years. Bethune's advice is common-sense leadership, with a focus on the customer, not the internal costs and finances of operating a business. Worthwhile reading for anyone trying to change the culture of their business into one focused on the ultimate barometer of success: creating loyal customers.

Peter Block, *The Answer to How Is Yes: Acting on What Matters.* This is a splendid book, detailing the importance of starting with *why* questions rather than *how* questions when confronted with any change. Anyone involved in changing people's minds needs to read this illuminating and lucid book.

David Boyle, *The Sum of Our Discontent: Why Numbers Make Us Irrational.* This very well-written work, which I read five years ago, had such a profound influence on my thinking it inspired me to write *this* book. It is an excellent history of counting and measuring and includes the 10 Paradoxes of Counting, which helped me shape my Seven Moral Hazards of Measuring, in Chapter 15. Highly recommended.

Christopher Cerf and Victor Navasky, *The Experts Speak: The Definitive Compendium of Authoritative Misinformation.* This book dispels any illusions one might have about the ability of anyone to predict the future, especially so-called experts. An educational and entertaining read.

Clayton M. Christensen, et al., *The Innovator's Solution: Creating and Sustaining Successful Growth;* and *Seeing What's Next: Using the Theories of Innovation to Predict Industry Change.* Christensen is one of the few management thinkers who understands the importance of utilizing theory in the embryonic discipline of management science, and these two books are excellent examples of the usefulness of positing, testing, falsifying, and advancing theories in business. With more thinkers like Christensen, the discipline of management might some day reach parity with economics.

Stephen R. Covey, *The 8th Habit: From Effectiveness to Greatness.* In this follow-up to his classic *The 7 Habits of Highly Effective People,* Covey provides a framework I believe is relevant to knowledge workers, even if a bit dense and convoluted. Though I remain unconvinced by some of his arguments, such as his "5 ages of civilization"—from hunter/gatherer, agricultural, industrial, information/knowledge worker, to wisdom—which makes it sounds as if there was no wisdom prior to modern times (what about Aristotle, Adam Smith, etc.?), Covey does a wonderful job focusing on doing the right things (effectiveness) rather than doing things right (efficiency).

Thomas H. Davenport, *Thinking for a Living: How to Get Better Performance and Results from Knowledge Workers.* We are going to need more books like this and more thinkers like Davenport if we are going to keep Peter Drucker's legacy alive of increasing the effectiveness of knowledge workers. The fact that there are so many disagreements over the definition of a knowledge worker, their optimal working environment, how to manage them, among other points of contention, vivifies how much work is left to be done.

Peter F. Drucker. Drucker is one of the truly serious thinkers the management consultant industry can point to with justifiable pride. Read anything and everything by Drucker. Even though he passed away November 11, 2005, at age 95, it does not mark the beginning of the end, but the end of the beginning, since he has left such a rich legacy. It is too bad the Nobel Prize is not given posthumously, because he certainly deserved one. For excellent one-book summaries of his life's work, see *The World According to Peter Drucker,* by Jack Beaty, and *Peter Drucker: Shaping the Managerial Mind,* by John E. Flaherty.

Richard Florida, *The Rise of the Creative Class: And How It's Transforming Work, Leisure, Community and Everyday Life;* and *The Flight of the Creative Class: The New Global Competition for Talent.* Florida is another thinker contributing to the knowledge worker topic, though he labels it the creative class. While I have serious doubts about some of his proposals with respect to government "investing" in furthering creativity, his books are thought-provoking expositions of this important sector of the workforce, providing a global perspective on the coming competition for this type of talent.

David D. Friedman, *Hidden Order: The Economics of Everyday Life*. David Friedman is Milton and Rose Friedman's son and an outstanding economist from Santa Clara University. This book is an excellent and engaging read.

George Gilder, *Recapturing the Spirit of Enterprise;* and *Wealth and Poverty: A New Edition of the Classic*. In my opinion, Gilder is the best writer and thinker on economics, sociology, technology, and entrepreneurship that you will find. I discovered his work, *Wealth and Poverty,* in 1981, and it forever altered my vision of the way the world works. These two books are his classics, but he has written many others. If you read only one book from this entire list, read anything by Gilder, twice. Gilder is a Senior Fellow at Seattle's Discovery Institute (www.discovery.org).

H. Thomas Johnson and Robert S. Kaplan, *Relevance Lost: The Rise and Fall of Management Accounting*. An indictment of the management accounting profession and how it has lost relevance in terms of helping businesses measure the right things. The book launched the activity-based costing movement, and is also a historically fascinating read.

H. Thomas Johnson, "Reflections of a Recovering Management Accountant"; and *Profit Beyond Measure: Extraordinary Results through Attention to Work and People*. The first is an excellent paper Johnson delivered that especially resonated with me since I, too, consider myself a recovering accountant. The second is the book that is Johnson's study of the legendary Toyota (and Scania) production process, all done without a standard cost accounting system, as discussed in Chapter 13. I believe both of these works are seminal, and will further the debate between managing by results versus managing by means.

Steven E. Landsburg, *The Armchair Economist: Economics and Everyday Life;* and *Price Theory and Applications, 5th ed.* Like David Friedman, Landsburg is an incredibly brilliant economist, besides being an excellent and enjoyable writer. He will no doubt challenge, and in many cases persuade, you with his cogent analysis of contemporary issues. To read Landsburg's "Everyday Economics" columns, go to www.slate.com.

Michael Lewis, *Moneyball: The Art of Winning an Unfair Game*. The parallels between Lewis's book and the arguments made in this one are uncanny, as Ed Kless's sidebar in Chapter 10 illuminated. The conventional measures in baseball are not predictive of team success, and it took an outsider—Harvard economist Bill James—to prove why. In fact, "conventional wisdom" in baseball is still resisting his hypothesis, which corroborates the history of how long it takes a new theory to diffuse into a given population—

decades, if not centuries. This book provides an apt sports metaphor on the importance of measures being guided by a theory. Even if you are not a baseball fan—and I'm not—this is an astonishing book. For those readers who want a more thorough analysis of Bill James, see *The Mind of Bill James: How a Complete Outsider Changed Baseball,* by Scott Gray.

Stanley Marcus, *Quest for the Best; The Viewpoints of Stanley Marcus: A Ten-Year Perspective; Minding the Store: A Memoir;* and *Stanley Marcus from A to Z: Viewpoints Volume II.* Stanley Marcus, the son of one of the founders of Neiman-Marcus, ran the store during the Great Depression until the late 1960s. I consider him the leader in customer service, and the many stories and examples in these works support this view. An amazing man and a great life story.

John Micklethwait and Adrian Wooldridge, *The Witch Doctors: What Management Gurus Are Saying and Why It Matters.* This piercing work—by two editors from *The Economist*—gave voice to the backlash against the $100-plus billion profession known as "consulting." Although the authors bestow far too much power on the consultants in altering the course of life, referring to them as "the unacknowledged legislators of mankind," their four defects of the "witch doctors" of our age are entirely accurate. The profession has yet to refute successfully the charges against it, so eloquently laid out in this book. For all those who have suffered through many a poorly written business book, Micklethwait and Wooldridge offer a refreshing alternative.

Henry Mintzberg, *Mintzberg On Management: Inside Our Strange World of Organizations;* and *Managers Not MBAs: A Hard Look at the Soft Practice of Managing and Management Development.* Mintzberg is Cleghorn Professor of Management Studies at McGill University in Montreal, Canada. If you ever thought our business education—especially the MBA—is dysfunctional, you will find Mintzberg's work compelling. The second work is especially relevant, and Mintzberg, like Clayton Christensen, is another management thinker who understands the importance of theory.

Eugene O'Kelly, *Chasing Daylight: How My Forthcoming Death Transformed My Life.* This may seem like a peculiar book to suggest, but I found it profound. I knew the author: he was a partner in the same office I was at Peat, Marwick, Mitchell (now KPMG) in the mid-1980s. In the last week of May 2005, at the age of 53, he was told he had three months to live. When he consulted another specialist on how long he had, the doctor replied: "You're not a statistic." What is fascinating is how O'Kelly, who went on to become CEO of KPMG—the international accounting firm and one of the Big Four—changed his perspective on evaluating people from competency, proficiency, and quality to the *energy* with which someone puts into a task. He admits he could have limited his office schedule, spent more time with his family, and probably been *more* focused and creative at work, and gotten more done. This is especially relevant to increasing the effectiveness of knowledge workers, and I hope we have the wisdom to learn from it—and practice it—without having to wait for a fatal diagnosis.

David Whyte, *Crossing the Unknown Sea: Work as a Pilgrimage of Identity*. Another unusual book to include, especially since Whyte describes himself as a corporate poet. Yet what he has to say about work is especially relevant to knowledge workers, hence I believe worth reading. He is also a terrific writer.

Lin Yutang, *The Importance of Living*. If you enjoyed reading the epigraph at the beginning of this book, you will thoroughly enjoy this classic. Superbly written and an enchanting read.

INDEX